BOOK DISPLAYS
A LIBRARY EXHIBITS HANDBOOK

ANNE C. TEDESCHI

WITH JANE PEARLMUTTER

FOR

THE CENTER FOR THE BOOK

AT THE

WISCONSIN ACADEMY OF
SCIENCES, ARTS AND LETTERS

D1520578

HIGHSMITH PRESS HANDBOOK SERIES

Fort Atkinson, Wisconsin

Published by Highsmith Press LLC
W5527 Highway 106
P.O. Box 800
Fort Atkinson, Wisconsin 53538-0800

© Wisconsin Academy of Sciences, Arts and Letters, 1997.

Cover by Mary Ann Highsmith.

All rights reserved. Printed in the United States of America.
Except as permitted under the United States Copyright Act of 1976, no part
of this publication may be reproduced or distributed in any form or by any
means, or stored in a database or retrieval system, without the prior written
permission of the publisher.

The paper used in this publication meets the minimum requirements of
American National Standard for Information Science —
Permanence of Paper for Printed Library Material. ANSI/NISO Z39.48-1984.

Library of Congress Cataloging-in-Publication Data

Tedeschi, Anne.
    Book displays : a library exhibits handbook / Anne C. Tedeschi with
  Jane Pearlmutter for The Center for the Book at the Wisconsin
  Academy of Sciences, Arts and Letters.
      p. cm. – (Highsmith Press handbook series)
    ISBN 0-917846-53-2 (paper : alk. paper)
      1. Library exhibits. 2. Library exhibits–United States.
  I. Pearlmutter, Jane. II. Wisconsin Academy of Sciences, Arts and
  Letters. III. Title. IV. Series.
  Z716.3.T43   1997
  021.7–DC20   96-34606

Contents

Preface

Most libraries display their new books throughout the year, but surprisingly few libraries turn these displays into real exhibits that support their general and special library programs. Few librarians see book exhibits as a way to contribute to their library's primary mission. This manual offers guidelines that will help a library to plan, prepare and execute an exhibit program to promote its collections and the library's desired image, as well as extend an educational and cultural influence into the community it serves.

While this handbook is designed primarily with the medium-sized library in mind, the coverage of subject matter will be consistent with any well-produced exhibit, to be made more elaborate or simplified to suit whatever an individual library may be able to afford. Since cost is a major factor for every library, these guidelines are intended to be practical and flexible, but sufficient to produce a professional book exhibit. This handbook includes sources for everything from exhibit cases to designs for in-house constructions, insurance guidelines and publicity.

Because this book is intended for the middle size library the most expensive equipment and plans have been left out deliberately. However, the bibliography reflects resources suitable for large institutional exhibitions. This manual offers practical suggestions on technical matters, such as mounting an exhibit or security and insurance, as well as innovative use of the exhibit format. A glossary and sources for equipment, supplies, services and further reading on exhibits will be found in the appendices.

LIBRARIES, THE REPOSITORIES OF OUR AMASSED INTELLECTUAL INFORMATION, BY CHOOSING SPECIFIC POLICIES AND PROGRAMS, AFFECT SIGNIFICANTLY THE LEVEL OF ACCESS TO THEIR MATERIALS

What book exhibits can do for a library

Book displays should be viewed as an important cultural and interpretive intellectual method for any educational institution, big or small. An exhibit program can be a major strategy in attracting the attention and reflecting the interests of a library's natural community, for presenting the image the institution wants to project, as a community hub, as an information resource, as a source of continuing education and cultural enrichment, or, all of these together. Book exhibits can play an important role in a library's mission to educate, and to extend knowledge into the community. For many libraries, this goal is primary, and exhibits that teach, even add to knowledge by drawing together ideas, sources, reference materials and much more, can have lasting influence. By fostering the use of books, drawing in a public that may otherwise not use the library, helping to establish links to community and to professional groups, and providing a tool for fund-raising activity, library exhibits offer substantial benefits.

BOOK EXHIBITS CAN BE A MAJOR STRATEGY IN ATTRACTING THE ATTENTION OF A LIBRARY'S NATURAL COMMUNITY

Art museums have long understood the power of imaginative exhibition strategies: no longer are paintings merely lined up in rows. The use of historical background material, beautifully designed settings, related lecture programs and visiting artists-scholars, gala receptions and other devices have helped bring unprecedented crowds to museums. Cooperatively developed traveling shows create excitement even before they reach their destinations, and reflect on their host institutions half a world away.

Major libraries such as the New York Public Library, the Huntington Library in California and the Harold Washington Public Library in Chicago have already taken up many of these strategies. But even in a smaller venue, libraries can tap into this vigorous approach. Often, the methods, devices and attitudes of large institutional libraries and museums can be translated into appropriate programs for smaller institutions. Library exhibits can be varied and imaginative, serious or fun, large or small, just books or of many different materials, but with planning, this can significantly contribute to a library's goals and reputation.

How does one decide just what exhibits are worth to a library? What priority should they be given in relationship to other important areas of concern such as patron access and collection development? Think for a moment of the library as a worthwhile commercial enterprise that must sell a product. It is not enough to create the product and maintain it. A library must "sell" their public on the "products" in its collection. Libraries must advertise. Without advertising, many people will not take the trouble to find out exactly what a library contains, or determine the importance of its collections, not only in general, but to themselves in particular. Exhibits can help make it happen.

Acknowledgments

For all the generous help in gathering information about library materials exhibitions, and providing charts, catalogs, brochures and slides, I am indebted to the following:

Erika Erickson, Exhibitions Preparator, the Huntington Library, San Marino, CA

Ruth Hamilton, Exhibitions Director, The Newberry Library, Chicago, IL

Ginny Moore Kruse, Director, The Children's Cooperative Book Center, The School of Education, The University of Wisconsin-Madison

Ken Sawyer, Reference Librarian, Jesuit-Krauss-McCormick Library, Chicago, IL

Pam Stuedemann, Department of Imaging and Technical Services, Art Institute of Chicago, Michigan at Adams, Chicago, IL

Susan Taraba, Exhibitions Coordinator, Department of Special Collections, University of Chicago, Chicago, IL

Marvene Williams, Center for the Book, The Library of Congress, Washington, DC

Thanks goes to the Madison area libraries which have allowed me to photograph their public spaces:

Middleton Public Library, Middleton, WI

Madison Public Library

The Oscar Rennebohm Library, Edgewood College, Madison, WI

Memorial Library, University of Wisconsin-Madison

The Cooperative Children's Book Center, School of Education,
University of Wisconsin-Madison

Thank You!

Book Exhibits With a Purpose

Chapter One

In order to put together an effective exhibit plan, a library needs to gather information about itself and its community. This chapter takes a look at the library's intended audience, user preferences, trends, and library service goals. It examines the staff and material resources, both physical and financial, that are needed to support the program of choice as well as offering tips for getting started on a basic program of book exhibits.

Review the library's goals

Before attempting to put together a plan for book exhibits, take the time to review your library's mission and goals. Do they support the community you serve? By asking the basic question, Who does this library serve? you will be focusing on the most important element of your exhibit plan: the audience your exhibits will reach or hope to reach. And since exhibit themes vary widely, it is always important to know what you them want to achieve and to remain focussed on primary goals.

Looking at readership trends helps identify themes based on timely subjects: What is most popular with different age groups? What circulates rarely? You may choose to build your exhibit around a popular genre, a political or social topic of timely significance to your community, or a special artistic or musical event; all or any of which you might be able to pinpoint by looking at these trends. Equally, you might want to take a look at little-used materials that may have hidden merit once attention is drawn to them.

Circulation figures may suggest other possibilities as well: if newspapers are heavily used, for example, this may point to a group of users with leisure time such as seniors who are retired, or there may be unemployment in the area that is bringing people to the library to use the newspapers for job hunting. The library has a lot of resources that might be of use to either of these groups, and exhibits can be a way of bringing vital information to the fore, on everything from health services, job training to free social and recreational events.

Another important group of users to consider in your planning is children. Exhibits for children have lately come into their own with children's museums leading the way. Exciting subjects such as marine life, with all the slimiest creatures, and outer space and robots have tended to take the place of more traditional displays. Well-crafted library exhibits can be crucial to this group: not only in order to help children find what they already know they want to read about, but in living up to the permanent responsibility of providing a balanced approach to information that will make sure our young people grasp the importance and joy of reading widely in our age of instant entertainment and sound bites.

Ethnic groups in your community have special interests and needs to consider in your planning—and may also provide a unique resource for you to draw on. Ethnic literature is a subject area of library acquisition that is fast becoming well developed, even in smaller libraries. Exhibits related to these materials can be some of the most visually exciting of all, and can offer an opportunity to use borrowed artifacts along with the print materials, encouraging ethnic members of the community to take active roles helping in library programs.

Some user groups may not be as visible as others: for example, does your library serve a particular professional community? Many libraries do, providing medical and legal information, or housing government documents. Materials connected to the history of the professions are quite common: a local donor may have given a personal collection of books and papers shaped by his or her career. Such collections are used infrequently, but when they are, often it is because there is no other easily available source for that precise information. These materials may be obscure to the uninitiated public but can be particularly appropriate for exhibit, as well as providing that special link to specific interest segments of the community.

Certainly one of the primary goals of most libraries is to further the cause of education, to bring knowledge within the grasp of their patrons. Exhibits can play a vital role in this respect, regardless of their size or scope. While some exhibits can be humorous and just for fun, and others be basically recreational in character, libraries should look for ways to develop information to act as a conduit to the depths and breadth of the subjects chosen.

Libraries generally serve some portion of a student or academic population. These are usually easy for a library to define: elementary school libraries serve the level of student in the school, seminary libraries serve students and scholars of religion, and so forth. If it is most important that an exhibit program be linked to academic courses, for example, then that should be a primary and permanent goal and a continuing element in exhibition planning.

Special libraries, while focussing first on their internal community, usually also serve a wider public, whether it be through reciprocal privileges with other institutions, a national constituency through a particular field or profession, or merely the local community at large, and exhibition themes should reflect this. Equally, general libraries and public libraries serve the specialized intellectual interests of their communities too, and have the responsibility to extend in-depth resources.

Literacy is a strong focus for many libraries today. The Library of Congress Center for the Book has a national campaign channeled through their state centers highlighting reading themes, including several traveling exhibits and a calendar of special nationally observed days for books and reading. The American Library Association also supports vigorous traveling exhibit and reading programs. Local literacy groups can build on these, using them in conjunction with their own lecture and study programs to reach out to an element of our public still struggling to read.

Most communities incorporate other educational and cultural institutions, such as art centers, hospitals that have instructional programs for the public, small art galleries, music schools, and other training centers. Libraries can reach out, helping to provide a support system for their educational endeavors. Cooperative exhibitions are exciting community events that can be a source of excellent family involvement, and draw many different kinds of learners together.

Evaluate where you are now

After doing a careful survey of your users and and the library's major service goals, you will want to review displays and exhibits you have done recently before embarking on planning a new or revised program. Take a close look at your library's past promotional events and the exhibits and activities tied to them. This includes reviewing not only the exhibits themselves but staffing, design and research skills available in-house, funding resources and equipment. If no records were kept in the past, tuck that fact away for later: good record-keeping has its uses. If there are a few remnants of old exhibits around, these can sometimes help to decide what the new plan ought to take into consideration. Make sure you cover the three questions here:

What have past exhibits been about?   Draw up a list of those you can remember in the last two years so that a new program will not repeat these themes or subjects too soon. Keep this up-to-date, so that future exhibit teams will have a good idea of what has occurred and will not have to start all over again. Look at those exhibits that were particularly successful and ask why. This examination may reveal another reason why exhibits should be well planned: all take time and money, if only in staff time. Well-planned and carefully stored exhibits with good records may be shown over again through the years, or used later to create cooperative exhibitions with other libraries.

What kind of exhibit spaces are available right now?   The answer will dictate what kind of an exhibit you can hope to plan at the moment. Examine the exhibit areas. Remember that the main purpose is to emphasize the availability of the library's materials; the display area must be welcoming and attractive. Good lighting is important. Are there some unused spaces that could be put to good use for exhibitions? In chapter 3, some ideas concerning exhibit spaces will be discussed.

What exhibit equipment does your library own?   Most smaller libraries have one or two exhibit cases; some larger institutions may have quite a few. They may be of a wide variety—standing cases, open stands, closed, glassed-in flat cases or merely a series of table-top cardboard props. How were items displayed in these cases? Does your library own any book supports or stands?

BOOKS GIVE US WINGS

Fig. 1.1. Books Give Us Wings is the logo of the Center for the Book, established in the Library of Congress to improve public awareness of books, reading and libraries. Supported by contributions from individuals and corporations, the Center sponsors events, programs, and exhibits at the Library of Congress and throughout the nation. A majority of states have established Centers for the Book, which are affiliated with the Center at the Library of Congress. A good example is the Wisconsin Center for the Book at the Wisconsin Academy of Sciences, Arts and Letters. For additional information on the Center for the Book and the state affiliates, call 202/707-5221. (Logo used courtesy of the Center for the Book, Library of Congress.)

Creating an exhibit team

What skills will team members need to have?

Many small libraries have only a few full-time staff members and usually a number of part-time workers, student help or regular volunteers. In this handbook, they will all be referred to as "staff." Regardless of the hours spent in the library, or the level of authority, any regular library worker can play a significant part in exhibition planning and preparation. The number of people on the team and some of the tasks required will vary with the type and subject matter of the exhibit, but some basic skills are general and will be useful most of the time.

Information gathering   Anyone with previous research experience or the love of digging into a subject, tracking down details and information would be a natural asset to your program. Reference librarians come easily to mind in this category.

Writing skills   Ideally, the same person might have the ability to create both captions for the exhibit and text for any publicity or publications. But if this is not the case, the task can be performed by another person willing to cooperate with the researcher. In any case, identifying someone with this skill is essential. Poor or incomplete captions and catalog text in a book exhibition will give the exhibit a feeling of amateurism— even when the books themselves are of great interest and worthy of an outstanding display.

A sense of design   Another necessary skill for exhibit work is a sense of design, both graphic and spacial. Graphic elements will appear in your exhibition, but will also be a critical part of any publicity or publications that are created for the exhibit. Spacial design is important in regard to the display itself. The visual impact in the layout of a book exhibition cannot be overemphasized: dull rows of books will attract virtually no attention. If no member of the library's permanent staff has a flair for the visual—color, line and form—try contacting a volunteer or a local person in the arts community for their input. More about design later.

Materials conservation   Collections with older, fragile items, documents or multimedia materials may require various amounts of conservation treatment before being exhibited. If a staff member is interested in conservation, book repair and collection maintenance, they should be encouraged to take a workshop or attend a conference to develop skills in this area. Book and document conservation cannot usually be learned well from manuals: book structure is always more complicated than is at first apparent. Materials can be permanently damaged by the wrong treatment or repair. It is also possible to contract an outside conservation facility for individual items. Materials to be exhibited that are poor condition should ideally be repaired *before* being placed on exhibit, rather than afterwards as further damage usually will occur from handling and from being exposed to varying environmental stresses. This is another area that will be covered again later.

Installation   Last, but not least, you will need a preparator, or someone who can install the materials neatly and safely, which is vital for any display of

Look for Special Skills
In an exhibition at the University of Chicago in the 1970s, it was necessary to erect small cases of already-mounted butterflies on an upright panel along with books showing studies and illustrations of the subject matter. This meant construction of book supports of varying sizes as well as supports for the butterfly cases. Because this was a private collection, the need for new research was minimal and information for the captions was supplied; construction and mounting became the only difficult aspects of creating the exhibition.

more than a few items. This person may also be able to handle design, repair or conservation treatments, but sometimes quite different skills come in handy, such as carpentry, in constructing cases and supports of all kinds, and a knowledge of materials such as papers, textiles, types of foam backing and board, is helpful.

HAVE AT LEAST ONE LIBRARY STAFF PERSON ON THE EXHIBIT TEAM TO PROVIDE CONTINUITY OVER TIME

Setting up the exhibit team

With some of the skills in mind that are required in exhibiting library materials, it is now possible to assemble an exhibit team or committee. A team may consist of two or more persons, be drawn from library staff or brought in as volunteers, either from existing volunteer groups, or sought out in relation to the theme of the exhibit itself for specific skills that might be needed. The obvious advantage of a team is the sharing of responsibilities and the minimizing of major disruptions in regular library services.

This "team" can vary with each individual exhibit, or it can be permanent. In either case, it is essential to have at least one library staff person on the team to act as exhibit coordinator and take basic responsibility for the initial planning, providing continuity over time. This person can keep track of equipment and supplies, and assign work on the exhibit at hand when necessary. If a library is really fortunate, this person may have all the skills necessary to put together an exhibit and install it too. In very small exhibits or what will be termed mini-exhibits in this book (of approximately ten to fifteen books or documents), this is usually the case.

Even for fairly sizeable exhibits, the team does not have to be large. For an exhibit on Equatorial Africa at the University of Wisconsin, the assistance of a part-time library worker was obtained on a volunteer basis. A person with conservation skills, she was able to construct some special supports for several unusual artifacts, as well as help to install the books in the cases. A faculty member acting as "curator" and a library staff liaison person, with some clerical help, completed the team for an exhibit of over one hundred pieces and fourteen cases.

Friends of the Library and volunteers

One of the very best fonts of talent and skill among volunteers in most libraries is the Friends of the Library group, or in cases where none exist, the library board. For smaller libraries that do not have such a group, an exhibit, especially one that has some community activity associated with it, may offer the chance to start one. By encouraging interest in a specific theme, volunteers can be urged to work with library staff to create exciting exhibits and then to link them with a social or community event.

If a friends group or board already exists, but does not do volunteer work in the library, exhibits are a good way to get them started. Museums, because they are visually exciting places, have little trouble recruiting volunteers but libraries do not as easily attract such attention. The jobs assigned to volunteers in libraries are often routine: dusting books, sorting cards, typing forms. Exhibits, instead, can be very exciting to work on; over a month or two of gathering the materials, planning handouts, researching information on a given subject, and getting ready for an author's talk, anticipation builds and bonds are formed that can grow into a permanent volunteer core—some-

Be Innovative

Sometimes innovative strategies can draw volunteers into exhibit planning. One such exhibition resulted from a survey on adults' favorite children's books. Twenty-five responders were invited to help create an exhibit around the theme.

thing every library needs in these days of shrinking budgets.

Volunteers can, in fact, do all the exhibit work, with the general oversight of a library staff member as coordinator. This is an excellent arrangement, as long as the standards for the quality of the exhibition are kept high. It is the library's responsibility to build into the exhibit plan a quality control system that delivers attractive, professional exhibitions.

The invited curator

In larger institutions, or in the case of the exhibition of a substantial subject-oriented collection there is often a "curator" invited or chosen—someone who takes the major responsibility for the planning and research. This may be a person outside the regular staff who has special expertise in the specific subject or collection. In an academic setting, it may be a faculty member; in the instance of a private collection, it is usually the owner of the materials, or it may be an invited person with special knowledge. The curator of an exhibit usually works with the library exhibit coordinator or team and produces the text for the captions and publications.

If a major exhibition is contemplated and the undertaking is outside the scope of the library's immediate staff, but will be adequately funded, a contractual arrangement with a curator could be considered. This might be in connection with a borrowed exhibit in which a designated courier follows the materials from site to site, or it might be a private arrangement by your library. In the latter case, after choosing and inviting a person who has particular knowledge and skills to bring to the job, a contract would be drawn up to set out the duties and expectations, time tables and scope of the exhibition. Unless the person is acting in a volunteer capacity, this greatly increases the cost of the exhibition. If grant or corporate funding is sought in advance, the costs of the contractual arrangement can be built in from the beginning.

Fund-raising for and with an exhibit program

Another possible goal of exhibit work in libraries is fund-raising. It is often hard to explain to prospective donors or financial contributors just what is so thrilling about book exhibits unless the library happens to own a famous work such as a *Nuremberg Chronicle* or a first edition of *Gone With the Wind.* Fund-raising is a traditional role for friends groups, library trustees and boards, but it is a difficult one. Big universities can use their football team to create enthusiasm, art museums can display striking art pieces and very visibly exciting shows, but few average libraries have many books that are so outstanding in themselves that they make the front pages of the newspaper, or the top of the morning TV talk show. Here again, innovative exhibitions provide a way of focussing attention on the real wealth of a library—its collections and the depth of knowledge they offer. Books in general may not get the immediate attention of the local community, but sometimes an exhibit tied to a stimulating theme can be the vehicle that does the trick. Once interest in the library is achieved, a continued exhibit program can be used to support further benefits and money-raising projects.

INNOVATIVE EXHIBITIONS PROVIDE A WAY OF FOCUSSING ATTENTION ON THE REAL WEALTH OF A LIBRARY— ITS COLLECTIONS

Exhibits can play a significant role in helping the public become aware of the library's practical needs as well: such things as funding for equipment, acquisition of materials and collection or building care. For example, if your library needs help to preserve specific items, consider framing an exhibit around these, showing the damage that needs correcting, exhibiting the tools used by bookbinders and conservators in repairing library materials, illustrating the hard life many circulating library books have on the "outside."

If your library has a strong Friends group, it may be able to support some aspect of an exhibit program, such as receptions and lectures. In turn, the exhibits can become a way of raising money and recruiting members. Local support for friends groups can translate into cooperative events as well: a visiting author making a presentation at a coffeehouse bookstore can give a lecture at the library as well when he or she is in town. The bookstore newsletter might be asked to publicize the Friends of the Library event—or a cosponsored event might be planned. A cooperative "Run/Walk for Literacy" offers still another tie for the libraries and the community—and possible exhibit theme. Exhibitions can become a very important part of the library's overall strategy for support from the community.

In one town, an "Open House of Private Collections" was arranged by the Friends of the Library as a benefit for a college library. A few weeks before the event an exhibit was opened in the library. It was made up entirely of large, standing screens covered with very large blow ups of beautiful title pages and illustrations from items that would be seen at the private homes. Captions were added that were designed to whet the appetite of the community and encourage early ticket sales for the event. Ticket holders automatically became Friends of the Library for one year, receiving invitations to future lectures and exhibitions. Participants were able to view the books themselves in the private homes, where refreshments were served and brief explanations were given on the history of the materials and on how the owners had come to collect them. The tours ended at the library where several valuable books that had been donated for the event were auctioned off.

In another Friends event, a fall benefit "Gathering in an Autumn Garden" was planned in an entirely out-of-doors setting in a small botanical garden. Participants were led through the garden and treated to literary allusions to the flowers and plants by a well-known horticulturist who had herself created a "literary" garden. Champagne and other refreshments were served and appropriate music was included. Participants were asked for a "donation" to the Friends of the Library. While this benefit was not accompanied by an exhibition, it would have offered a perfect event around which one might have been planned far enough in advance to act as advertisement, gaining maximum awareness for the library and its "garden" literature by the interested public, continuing community interest long after the event.

National funding sources such as the National Endowment for the Humanities have supported many exhibitions linked with conferences and other public programs including the traveling programs discussed in chapter 5. But for more modest endeavors, possibilities for small grants from local sources should not be overlooked: state and local historical societies, state library councils, clubs such as Kiwanis or Rotary, and corporate sponsorship.

Once your basic program planning is completed, you can go looking for outside and local support. Call first and make an appointment where possi-

Fig. 1.1. Many events can suggest exhibit themes. This poster and the fund-raiser it announces are ideally suited to combine with an exhibit on garden literature.

ble, and have your library literature as well as the exhibit program plan with you when you arrive. If your library does not have appropriate literature that outlines goals and events programs, this is the time to create some. See chapter 4 for suggestions on design and layout.

Choosing exhibit formats

There are many different kinds of exhibits and many different ways of promoting any given theme. In addition to the usual table with books laid out or supported by stands, or glass cases full of books, there are innovative methods of display, such as wall-mounted exhibits, standing screens, presentations that include hands-on elements, electronic devices, traveling exhibits that come partially assembled, to mention only a few. The ideas in this handbook are aimed at producing educational book exhibits developed around an intellectual theme, rather than quick, basic displays.

MANY MUTE DISPLAYS COULD BE TURNED INTO MINI-EXHIBITS WITH A MINIMUM OF EFFORT

Such displays, however, have their purposes and are already used regularly in most libraries. One good source for this type of exhibiting is found in *The Library Display Handbook* by Mark Schaefer. Here the librarian can learn how to create neat, attractive signs, and small, effective displays. A bibliography is included with more information on design and library displays, and a calendar of yearly holidays and events around which a library might plan interesting, lively themes for simple displays between larger book exhibitions.

Most smaller libraries have at least one large exhibit for case housing displays in the entrance area. But many are just that, displays, without much comment. With a minimum of effort these mute displays could be turned into mini-exhibits simply by adding other appropriate books and well-thought-out captions and background materials. Sometimes it is not the exhibit material itself, but the method of presentation that needs improvement. Cases that are too crowded or have captions that are too long and complicated often discourage viewers as much as those with too little material. Sometimes an interesting subject that has been well presented only needs some visually attractive color to draw an audience. Especially when a library has only one exhibit case, it is important to maximize the impact, both visual and intellectual, of the display.

Along with keeping the exhibit area neat, full and exciting, goes the variety of strategies that support and make exhibitions work. These might include cooperative ventures with other institutions, field trips linking exhibits with other community or institutional programs, workshops held at the library and many other devices more for consciousness-raising than for fund-raising.

Fig. 1.2. This table exhibit of marbled papers featured excellent research and good captions, but the design and layout needed help—it looked too crowded and jumbled to be attractive. With better background screens, book supports and a more spacious arrangement, it could have seemed more interesting. Would you stop to read these captions or does it look too complicated?

In planning an exhibition program for your library, it may be a good idea to study different exhibit formats first, to determine whether they may offer, not only a variety of ideas, but of costs. It may be that your library can afford one or two major book exhibitions planned and executed in-house in a year, and that the intervals between them could usefully be filled with simple displays available for more nominal costs, or by sharing expenses with other libraries.

Selecting exhibit themes

In selecting an exhibit theme, the natural place to look first is to your own library's collections. While it is instinctive to choose a subject that is currently popular with users, there needs to be balance throughout the exhibit program, reflecting the educational, recreational and cultural sides of a library's resources. In general you should consider the following:

Pick a subject that is not too general, that can be broken down into several significant aspects. It is usually easier to create a good exhibition from a relatively narrow and carefully defined subject.

Avoid small but heavily used subject areas in the library's collection. It should be taken into consideration that books on exhibit are not available to patrons. Limited materials may be a poor choice for exhibition since it will be frustrating for patrons to find many similar-subject items out of reach over a three month exhibit period.

Look at older, less used materials. Older libraries, those formed earlier than the 1950s, often contain much of their original collection, some of which will

Fig. 1.3. A small exhibit case at the Cooperative Children's Book Center, a library of the School of Education at the University of Wisconsin-Madison, featured an outstanding educational display that was the object of continual interest. Beautifully designed for a small space, the exhibit expressed the actual journey in the Newberry Award-winning novel *Walk Two Moons* by Sharon Creech. Other "journeys" were also included in the display: the journeys of both the book and the author after winning the Newberry Award, and the journey to Madison, as featured in the book. (Exhibit creators: Kathleen Horning and Robin Gibson; photographs: Ginny Moore Kruse.)

have become what is sometimes called "historical" and even occasionally may be rare. Some of these earlier materials may receive little use and are always in danger of being weeded. One strategy for retaining underused collections is to make them earn their keep: use of such items for exhibitions is a wonderful way to draw the attention of the library community to the depth and breadth of collections in general and reveal the unexpected strengths of some collections in particular, and sometimes, pressing preservation needs, including more space to house these at-risk collections.

Follow the lead of school or academic events. In an academic setting, current courses and events can help set a basis for exhibits throughout the school year, but equally, exhibitions themselves can act as catalysts for on-campus activities such as invited speakers, receptions and celebrations of new acquisitions in the library. Frequently, alumni/ae become donors to the library.

Use exhibits to teach. Most libraries already serve the school communities in their areas very well, and offer many events, especially in youth services. But exhibitions can be used as an additional educational tool. Relatively new library facilities often have large, underused areas that would make good exhibition space. Exhibit themes for heavily used areas could be tailored to mini-exhibits: each case could be a different aspect of one academic subject, or each case could be geared toward a specific school level, or each case could show outstanding work from different schools, including the library books that were used by the students in their research. Once or twice a year, these cases could be brought together for a more in-depth treatment of a specific theme or series.

Look around the community. Here the possibilities are almost endless: Exhibitions may be tied to local events, national or state themes such as centennials, the birth of a famous person or a holiday. Travel agencies, industry and businesses, anything to do with local history, ethnic and national issues, even the local newspaper can provide not only the ideas for exhibit programs, but the people who will be able and willing to help create them.

Borrow an exhibit. In visiting other towns and public buildings, or educational institutions, keep an eye out for displays that might suit your library. Even if another institution has not thought of having their exhibition travel, it is sometimes possible to arrange, particularly if your library has a well-organized routine in place that can offer competent help from your staff in taking down and setting up an exhibit, and provide materials security and insurance. A later chapter will explore borrowing and loaning library materials.

Consider an exhibit schedule. If your library has never had an exhibit program before, you should probably begin very modestly, two or three small exhibits in a year's time, especially if the equipment you have on hand is minimal. You may want to rent or borrow a few more cases to accommodate exhibits for a pilot venture before deciding to add or buy new equipment. You may just want to borrow simple displays while creating a more ambitious plan for the following year. However small or large the program, it is still vitally important to plan ahead. The next chapter will discuss planning and developing an exhibit schedule.

Expand a craft display into a teaching opportunity
In one library, a well-arranged, colorful display of crafts by local artists was set up in a large wall case in the outer lobby. This was an excellent idea but, although the artists and their pieces were identified, the display had no other information. To create a mini-exhibition, a few books on these arts and crafts might have been exhibited, and one or two large-type captions discussing some of the history or technical methodology to offer the viewer some insight to reading on the subject. The library might have produced a free information sheet about the artists themselves for viewers to take home.

The first steps, revisited

Create an exhibit team: Take stock of the skills of your available staff, whether they be full-time, part-time or volunteers. Decide whether it might be a good time to start volunteer or Friends of the Library programs.

Select one or more exhibition themes: Choose some basic subjects that complement the library's goals, and/or can be linked to already-in-the-works community or local activities. Pick fairly specific themes for the displays themselves.

Look into funding: Taking into account what sort of funding you might expect from the library, consider adding at least one or two exhibitions based on outside sources of financial support, especially if you do not have an adequate budget on which to draw. This will force you to use the exhibit program as a fund-raising tool and could help it become a support mechanism.

Decide on a time frame: Allow enough time for the exhibition themes to be developed carefully. Timing will depend not only on internal library schedules, but at least partially on basic funding and on the time available for library staff to seek further outside financial support.

Developing the Exhibit Plan

Chapter Two

Planning is the key to a successful exhibit program. In this chapter, budgeting and insurance, defining topics and researching them, support activities, timetables and more will be discussed. These are the parts of a complete exhibit program that should be considered by any library when creating a customized plan to fit targeted service goals.

MAXIMUM BENEFIT FROM AN EXHIBIT PROGRAM CANNOT BE REALIZED UNLESS IT IS TIED TO THE LIBRARY'S EVENT CALENDAR

Begin early

Even a modest book exhibit should be developed from some sort of a written plan. Certainly, if an ongoing program of exhibits to support your library's programs and enhance fund raising capabilities is desired, careful planning is necessary. Even for a single sizeable exhibit, planning needs to be based on at least a six-month timetable; to be truly cost efficient, it should encompass a year or more.

Your library will derive the maximum benefit from an exhibition program that is tied to the library's events calendar. By planning ahead, you may also be able to take advantage of cost sharing. For example, if your library is preparing to take part in a community event, such as a centennial celebration, the exhibit might be organized and directed by the same people who are centrally involved in the centennial event. The library might have an exhibit of popular music, literature and biographical materials of the period, while the local historical society could present another aspect of the same theme, displaying personal papers, books and artifacts of some early citizens. Cooperation can reduce costs considerably if the effort and expense of planning and mounting the exhibits are shared.

Another reason for planning exhibits as far into the future as possible is to allow other people and groups to plan events around the library's displays. With a theme set well in advance, school events, conferences and special events may be planned around it. Visiting-author events, or state-organized reading programs might tie into or be enhanced by local library exhibits. By adding to or stimulating additional events, a library gets increased mileage out of each exhibition.

Budgeting for a basic program

How were past exhibits funded in your library? Not many libraries have a budget line for exhibits. Usually funds are simply drawn as necessary from other areas such as supplies and equipment, and staff time is borrowed. It is, however, difficult to set up an ongoing exhibit program in this way. It means that other budget lines will continually and unevenly be tapped, and real exhibit costs will remain unknown. Worse, this approach yields an uneven quality in exhibits: an exhibition based on a private collection whose owner supplies almost everything may look very professional, while the next one, because nothing had been planned or budgeted, is hastily pulled together with little thought, with a boring or amateurish result.

SETTING A MINIMUM SUM FOR EACH EXHIBITION ALLOWS PLANNING TO GET STARTED; RAISING ADDITIONAL FUNDS MAY OCCUR LATER

To avoid these problems, add a separate budget line for exhibits, lectures and whatever else might be planned as accompanying programs. (Often this package of events undertaken by a library is termed "public programs.") In this way, everyone knows where things stand. Whatever arrangement you have, make sure good records of exhibit costs and funding are be kept. These actual expenses will be invaluable when creating future exhibition programs.

Ideally, some amount of funding should be delegated to each project on the exhibit calendar, that is, if an exhibit is desired every three months, or four are planned in a calendar year, a lump sum might be designated for each. For many libraries, this budget may be very limited, but it is at least a start. Begin with the question, How much is affordable right now?

The costs of each exhibit will differ depending on the size of the exhibit, the publicity and materials created to support it and the extended community events around the exhibit theme. For planning purposes, however, a modest basic budget can be assigned for each event, with the difference coming from supplementary funding sought for special purposes. This is where outside fund-raising comes in. For instance, the extra expense of printing a catalog might be donated by the printing firm, or be underwritten by a local publisher. Food for a reception might be provided by a member of the Friends of the Library or donated by a local grocery store. For a more ambitious exhibit that requires more extensive funding, or for a rented show, it may be better to seek the financial support for the entire event after it has been planned, from one or more corporate or private donors.

The initial purpose of setting a minimum sum for each exhibit in the program is that it allows planning for the program as a whole to get started. And, when seeking outside financial support, the existence of some library funding creates confidence in a prospective donor that the proposed program will in fact become a reality. Fund-raising for major exhibit programs is usually combined with the development needs of the library as a whole, at least when looking for corporate sponsorship or government support, so that a request for financial help is presented as a well-rounded and thought out total plan.

Scope and topic definition

After selecting a theme for a book exhibit, there are several steps that may be useful in forming the scope and depth of the show:

Choose a Simple Title   A title for an exhibit should indicate the reason these particular materials have been selected. A few general words can be chosen to begin with; subtitles may be added later to define the precise topic, especially as text for a poster: *The Pharmacist and Patient: The Preparation of Medicines Through the Ages*, or, *The Creative Process: The Manuscript, Publication and Design Materials of the Award-winning Children's Book* The Westing Game. A title may be used to bring forward a message: *What Can a Woman Do? American Women Writers Through the 19th Century*. Titles can easily be amended to be more concise and accurate after the topic is defined and finalized.

Fig. 2.1. Subtitles define what a viewer will expect to see in the exhibition.

Define the Scope of the Exhibit   Look at the range and quantity of materials that lend themselves to the chosen subject. The difficulty is not so much in finding enough materials for an exciting exhibit, but in deciding how to narrow down a wide scope of interesting materials to a clear concept that will lend itself to a significant message.

A Basic Formula: Identify several important aspects of your major subject and divide them evenly among the number of available exhibit cases. Then determine how many average books will fit into each case without crowding, leaving room for the number of captions you want to include.

This will give you a round number of books with which to start. Later, you can break the rules: one large book can equal two others; two cases can be used to cover an aspect of the subject that is more important than the others, or several artifacts may take the place of some redundant items.

For example

In a small exhibit on Harriet Beecher Stowe, you might decide to concentrate mainly on her life and influences on her. There will be four exhibit cases and approximately eight to ten books will fit into each case. Two cases will deal with her family and her youth, the next will be devoted to her education, friends and relatives during her productive years as a writer, and the last case with her impact on society from her own time until now. Books will take second place to letters and photographs in the first two cases, other books in addition to her own will be used in the last two cases. At this point, you have an approximate idea of how many items you can expect to use.

In a preliminary selection, it is entirely appropriate to choose somewhat more books and materials than will ultimately be exhibited simply because as the theme is defined and developed, and physical space tightens, you will have alternatives to use in filling any remaining holes in the case. For example, limited space may mean that a small book illustrating the same point must be found rather than a more obvious one that is too large for the case.

Although you will need to examine the actual materials during the selection process, they should not be pulled from the collection yet to avoid confusion for library staff and patrons. Since books on display are not available to patrons, it is not a good idea to keep large numbers of books and documents away from their assigned places for long periods before the exhibit even begins. Once the final selection has taken place, a list should be drawn up to be used by team members who may need temporary access in order to measure books for book stands and supports. Actual gathering of the physical items may not need to happen much before a few weeks in advance of installation: at that time, all materials should be charged out at the circulation desk.

The message: Research and text development

When the initial, tentative selection of materials has been made, decide how much additional information will be necessary for captions, publications or support activities.

Information Gathering   Research should now be assigned to one or more persons on the exhibit team, taking into consideration how long this phase should take. A basic introduction to the subject should be written, whether it is included in a brochure, becomes a longer essay in a catalog, or is merely blown up and included in the main exhibit case. Sometimes, for reasons of space and cost, catalogs do not include all the captions of items that are exhibited, but may add more in-depth annotations to the most important pieces.

Acknowledgments   This is the time to start keeping track of any people who will need to be thanked or credited in the catalog or in the exhibit, donors or lenders and those who may have offered their expertise. Do not forget protection for the library against liabilities for copyright violations. It is important to have a completed list of the exhibit items as early as possible in order that copyright restrictions, disclaimers, permissions for quotes, photographs and publicity may be sought where necessary, as well as any special dispensations for commercial use.

Captions   Occasionally, artifacts and books exhibited merely for their covers are not identified if the title and author are visible, or if they are mentioned generally in another caption, but most exhibited items should be accompanied by explanatory labels.

Some captioning suggestions

1.   Sometimes special information is needed as in the case of a photograph or painting credit or where special typefaces or formats need to be noted.

2.   If the item is from a private collection or loaned by an individual, it is imperative to include the person's name and the name, if any, of the collection.

3.   A caption may mention the source of the material, its importance to the group of books in the case or to a specific item, and to the exhibit as a whole as well as such things as previous editions, or the popular history of the book.

4.   Captions need to be fairly concise in spite of all the things that need to be included. Viewers will not pause to read long, involved explanations

Create a detailed exhibit list
In order to make a list of items useful to the exhibit team, descriptions should be quite detailed:

Include title, author, date and place of publication or photocopy the title page, as this information will be needed for captions.

Add a physical description: *"large leather volume, very heavy. Weak front cover and detached title page. Good map on p. 23. and interesting illustrations all together in the center."*

Indicate how the volume being included will serve in the exhibition: "...can be used to show early interest in female suffrage. Illustration of Susan B. Anthony p. 5."

If the item is not fragile, **photocopied maps or illustrations can be useful** to include with the list.

THE DIFFICULTY IS TO DECIDE HOW TO NARROW DOWN THE SCOPE OF INTERESTING MATERIAL TO FIT A CLEAR CONCEPT THAT WILL DELIVER AN IMPORTANT MESSAGE while moving through an exhibit. If longer explanations are required, they are better included in an annotated checklist or catalog.

5.   Captions may be made for each individual item or several items may be grouped in one. The proper caption format requires standard bibliographic information, especially if it is to be used in a catalog or other printed matter. The caption for a book should include the author, title and place and date of publication. When desired, the publisher may be included.

The following is an example of a standard caption and the publication information that should be included.

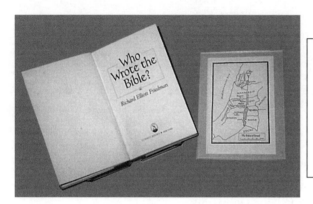

This interesting book is a dramatic re-appraisal of the Old Testament. A truly exciting work, it helps us relate the complex issues of our age to the most famous of all books, the Bible.

Map illustration, "The Tribes of Israel," p.9.

Friedman, Richard A., *Who Wrote the Bible?* New York: Harper & Row, 1987.

Social events and support activities

In an exhibition program, social events may be planned that draw attention to and significantly enhance the importance of any given exhibit. Lectures, readings, music and even field trips can lend an expanded meaning. Innovative events often captivate an otherwise casual audience: in connection with an exhibit on ancient magic, a library found a speaker who was also versed in the methods of medieval magic tricks and could demonstrate them; another exhibit on a Scandinavian country featured children dancing period pieces in costume. At the very least, the opening of a major new exhibition should be accompanied by some kind of event, reception or lecture to alert the community to the new material.

Film and Video

Supportive materials for library exhibitions may come from other media in the library, such as audio and video collections. Just as effective, though perhaps intended for a different audience, is an exhibition that has a video portion which can deliver the intellectual message, taking the place of a catalog. A computerized checklist of the items on exhibit may be available to guide the viewer from item to item instead of an entire catalog.

The device of film and video is widely used in museums. The use of video with book exhibits has been less used, but may have excellent applications for exhibitions that want to attract a wider audience. For example: In an exhibition on the theme of Christopher Columbus, the relevant printed materials of books and documents alone might not interest a young audi-

ence, but if the exhibition also included some artifacts such as nautical
devices, clothing of the period and good illustrative supports, a video
explaining the whole would help draw it together for this age group.

The ideal is to plan a lecture series or events that go with each exhibition planned. The public that is drawn to a first exhibition will begin to look
forward to interesting events that accompany the next one. Outside sponsorship for exhibitions is often a help, since it brings a built-in audience. Friends
of the Library is a natural one, but any community group, or groups can play
this role. If a library is planning four exhibitions in a year, each of the four
may be supported by an activity planned and paid for by a business or com-
munity-based group, such as a local Lions Club, or the Boy Scouts. For exhibitions with a specific subject matter, a sponsor may suggest itself and even
help to decide on an appropriate event: an exhibition on German-American
literature was supported by a German-American institute at a state university,
linked to a conference and successfully concluded with a reception for the
participants with the exhibit as the focal point.

Timetables: Create a calendar

When approximate exhibit themes and other events have been chosen, it is time
to get things in writing. Other events may dictate when a certain exhibition
needs to be up, but in some cases it may be purely a matter of balance. For exam-

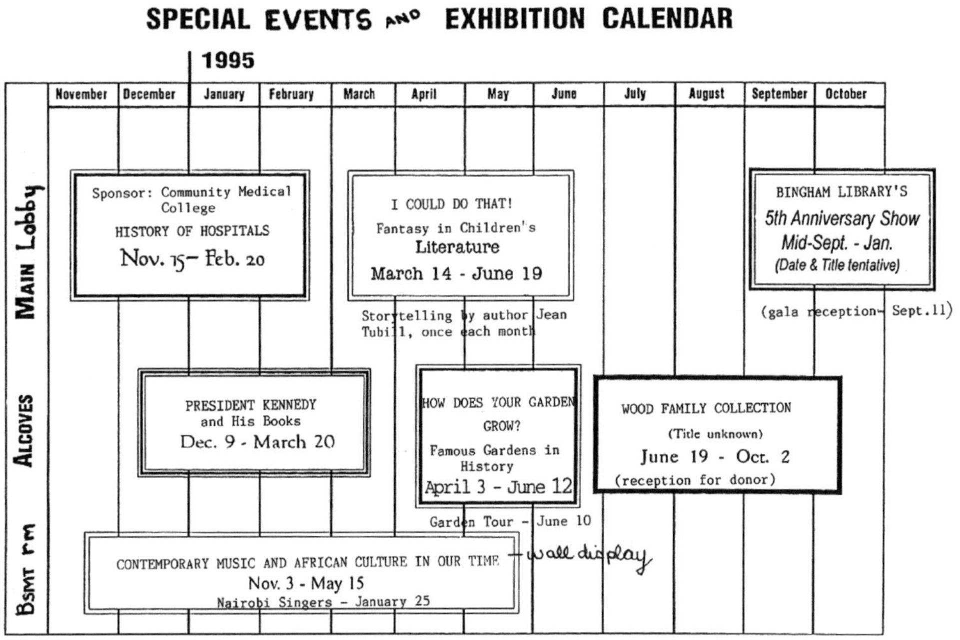

Fig. 2.2. Here is a mock-up of a proposed year's calendar of exhibitions and special events. Notice
that there are very few times when an exhibit of some kind is not in place. There are three different kinds of exhibitions represented here: the main lobby space for primary exhibitions, the
smaller upright cases in alcoves where mini-exhibitions can be shown, and the basement room that
is used for social events where minimal security wall exhibitions of posters, framed documents and
the like are set up. Special related events and sponsorship are typed in where known.

ple, if an exhibit of children's literature has been planned for the fall months, the winter holidays should probably try to feature something for adults.

A calendar of the library's exhibit plans is essential. As soon as possible, the exhibit coordinator should make up a tentative, single-page calendar that can be copied and distributed to all interested parties. Invite suggestions and comments about the timeliness of the exhibits and events shown, especially from library staff. Remember not to schedule openings or support events such as lectures on important holidays such as Easter or Hanukkah. As things change and are firmed up, the calendar may be easily revised and redistributed. Build in cut-off dates for finalizing the major content and scheduling decisions: something like three to six months in advance of the opening date. It is essential to keep all major players in the planning informed about any changes. Large libraries that have a program of continuous and substantial exhibitions find it most economical to plan two to five years in advance.

Publications: Catalogs, brochures and checklists

Exhibits often generate new demands on the library and its staff. This possibility should not be underestimated, and the library should be prepared for increased circulation of and curiosity about materials related to the exhibit. Publications can come in handy in meeting the need for information about exhibit materials: it is much easier to hand someone a well-prepared pamphlet describing the library's related holdings than to have a busy staff member take the time to recite them.

There are other reasons why a library may want to plan a publication program since exhibition catalogs, especially those having to do with the library's collections, can be excellent publicity tools and informative messengers. Merely the discipline of producing a catalog can help interpret and develop both the theme of the exhibition, its goals and the intended target audience. It is also preferable to have an exhibit easily understood visually, without resorting to long, hard-to-read captions in the exhibit cases. A catalog or other separate printed checklist will help satisfy the requirement of carrying the educational message to the viewing public.

Though exhibitions themselves are temporary, the exhibit catalog becomes a permanent educational tool. Not only does it publicize the library's holdings, but it may make an intellectual contribution in its own right. Catalogs may range from heavily annotated lists of items complete with scholarly introduction to a simple checklist of reproduced captions to guide the viewer through the exhibition. Catalogs may be elaborate, professionally published, with glossy illustrations, or inexpensive, simple, desk-top created, photocopied lists. Brochures and simple checklists may be used instead of a catalog or used as a free handout along with a catalog if the library needs to recoup the cost of the latter's publication by selling it. There is only one rule: catalogs or other guides must be produced **before** the exhibit opens! In chapter 4, several different approaches to creating well-designed publications will be examined.

Although most catalogs are based on the actual captions in the

Fig. 2.3. Interesting covers can turn these inexpensive desk-top produced lists of captions into catalogs which can become bibliographic and educational guides to your library. By adding more colors, and illustrations to an annotated text, they become very attractive.

exhibition itself, sometimes additional annotations are made, or an introductory essay is included. Some aspects that might add further interest to a catalog are:

> **Educational** The theme and viewpoint of the exhibit can be treated in depth, but other aspects can also be interesting. Contributions to scholarship by the materials in the exhibition could be noted. The items themselves also may be described as to their provenance, how and when they were made, physical attributes such as typefaces, bindings, and any unusual or unique properties that were not mentioned in the captions.

> **Historical interest** The historical importance of the materials as well as the background surrounding the theme of the exhibit itself is often of special interest. This is particularly true when exhibiting a private or single collection or a donor's books: How and why was this collection begun? What is its historical scope?

> **Bibliographical** Related holdings in the library may be listed to give the interested viewer a chance to dig more deeply into the exhibit subject. Items of particular rarity can be examined in more depth.

> **Acknowledgments** This is the place to mention donors of any exhibited pieces. A catalog may recognize special events too, such as an ethnic holiday to which an exhibit might be related, or an anniversary of the donation of a major collection.

Insurance and security risks

Last, but most certainly not least, the matter of insurance must be considered. As a very general approach, most libraries are insured to about 80 percent of the estimated value of the collection when it contains special materials of value or for what is considered "permanent" research materials. No matter what insurance a library has, it should be realized that items on exhibit are far more likely to be damaged or even stolen, especially where security is poor, equipment antiquated and supervision minimal. The most likely case is one where the humidity becomes so great that book covers are warped and mold develops. Or in the process of installation, a book may be dropped and broken, a page torn, a pamphlet lost. When an exhibition is loaned or borrowed, there are additional cautions that will be treated later in chapter 5, but any library intending to borrow library materials must review the level of security it offers.

The possibility of fire, water or natural disaster occurring should not be ignored: disasters do happen. Under such circumstances, all exhibited materials could be lost. In planning an exhibition program, it is a good idea to have a copy of the library's insurance regulations, requirements and compensation information among the planning documents. In a state or public institution, disaster is often handled by a central risk management office, and a list of exhibit materials sent to that office is sufficient for claims in the event of a disaster. Suffice it to say here, that attention to security risks and insurance coverage in the planning stage is important to avoid difficulties with the insurance company in the event of damage.

Libraries with a disaster plan for the building as a whole should make sure that exhibitions are specifically mentioned in it, since these materials are not in their usual locations. In addition, display materials are often particularly important to the collection as a whole, and even of greater monetary value, and in the event of a disaster, may warrant a high priority for salvage.

In general, the basic steps for planning exhibit insurance are:

1. Familiarize yourself with your library's insurance policies and coverage for damaged materials, and restrictions that might apply to exhibitions. Find out the steps to be taken to add a rider, or endorsement, to your library's normal coverage if it does not cover exhibitions. For a library exhibiting valuable materials, it is usually necessary to add a codicil to insurance coverage, allowing extra coverage for specific items. The coverage extends only for the period of the exhibit.

2. Have a complete list of all the items that will be displayed, whether library property or borrowed. This list must include a short description of the original condition of the item and an estimated total value for general materials, with individual values for special items.

3. Have a contact person at the insurance company to answer questions when needed.

4. Find out exactly how you report damage. For example, in some cases, an insurance company may require that a representative of the company actually see the damage, as might be the case after a fire. If there is such a restriction, taking photographs of the materials before the exhibition may be wise.

In the case of minor damage, under no circumstances should untrained library personnel try to "glue" broken items back together. This may create further problems. The damage should be documented, and when a trained book repair person is not available in the library, the item should be sent to a book and document conservation facility. In the case of a borrowed item, it is *imperative* that permission be received from the loaning institution and settlement with the insurers be achieved, before any repairs are undertaken. In chapter 3, conservation and book repair are discussed further, and ways for finding a conservator are suggested in the appendices.

Security

Different levels of security are needed for different types of exhibits, but in general, security should extend not only to the hours when the library is open and people are actively viewing the exhibit, but also during hours that the library is closed. Whenever possible, a major exhibition space should be located in a secure part of the building and not be, for example, in a lobby outside of the library proper, as in the case of some institutions where the library is part of a larger building. During the hours that an exhibit is open, active supervision of some kind should be available, not only when valuable items are on view, but also for standing displays, artifacts not enclosed in cases or items hung in corridors. If an exhibit includes any sort of a hands-on display, care must be taken that the display is safe for the public that will handle it, particularly if this includes children.

Evaluating the plan

Once a plan is completed, it is a good idea to evaluate each exhibit according to a list of specific criteria, so that all exhibits can be held up to the same basic standards and display the same level of professionalism. Here are some questions to ask:

Goals: Do the planned exhibitions in some central way support the goals of the library?

Scope: Do the exhibitions fit into the scope of the library's collections or enhance them in some way?

Theme: How does the subject matter for each exhibition educate? Are there enough appropriate materials for this subject?

Funding: How is each exhibition funded? Will funding come from the library entirely? Will outside funding be sought? Who is in charge of this aspect? Have all costs to do with technical matters been considered?

Staff: Who will be acting as exhibit coordinator of each exhibition? Will there be outside special assistance needed? How much library staff time will the program require? Have volunteers been recruited for help?

Audience: What precise audience will each exhibition attract? Is there a goal of reaching a particular audience? Will these exhibitions increase interest in and awareness of the library?

Support Activities: In what ways do the exhibitions enhance or are enhanced by supporting programs? Are there links to library or other community events? Does each exhibition have a publication attached to it? Are there any other media events possible or planned? Is publicity sufficient to warrant the time and effort?

Technical Matters: How much space will each exhibition require? Is equipment sufficient or will additional materials be necessary? How long will each exhibition be up? Have all matters such as publicity, publications, security, insurance, shipping and/or packing, borrowing and/or loaning and installation been taken into consideration?

Some of these questions will be discussed again in future chapters as we go along.

The Exhibit Program Document

At the end of the planning stage, in addition to the one-page exhibition events calendar, an internal document for the use of the exhibit team and library staff is recommended. This should set out all the major assignments connected to the calendar and set them in a time frame.

You will note on the Exhibition Schedule Checklist (see pp. 24–25) that planning for removing, repacking, reshelving and inspecting exhibited items once they come out of an exhibit is on the checklist. This is not an optional matter: many books and documents have been lost or damaged because they were carelessly removed or left sitting around after an exhibition.

EXHIBITION SCHEDULE CHECKLIST

	Contact Person	Date Completed
One year advance:		
Designate theme proposal, materials, exhibit coordinator and other jobs		
Choose publications and support events		
Four months prior to opening exhibit team meets to:		
Choose items to be exhibited		
Cover insurance, permissions, security, conservation and installation matters		
Define specifics for support events. Sign up for necessary facilities.		
Engage speakers or outside consultants		
Set publications deadlines		
Two months prior to opening meet to complete schedule for installation:		
Finalize approval of equipment, book supports, artifacts		
Approve final layout of items in display cases		
Review preliminary draft of captions		
Finalize drafts and dates for publications that will accompany exhibition		
Pick up posters or signage		
Check arrangements for support events:		
Accommodations for speaker		
Related community events		
Press releases, radio & TV announcements		
Two weeks before opening prepare for accompanying events:		
Food for reception		
Arrangements for speaker		
Pick up publications accompanying exhibit		
Print final captions		
Arrange for any cleaning or furniture arrangement of exhibit space		

EXHIBITION SCHEDULE CHECKLIST

	Contact Person	Date Completed
A few days before installation and opening:		
Clear and clean exhibit cases; prepare items for installation		
Make security and conservation check once items are installed		
Prepare area for opening reception or other event		
Exhibition closing:		
Removal and inspection of exhibited items		
Damage report		
Return of exhibited items to origin		

Technical Matters

Chapter Three

The technical aspects of book exhibits must be handled efficiently, not only in order that the display will have a professional appearance, but to help keep control of equipment and installation costs, and maximize the use of the library's space and personnel talents. In this chapter, exhibit spaces, equipment and supplies are examined, and preservation for the exhibited materials is covered, along with an examination of book supports, including a few designs that can be made in-house.

Exhibit spaces and equipment

While it is necessary to take into consideration your present exhibit space when planning begins so that exhibitions fit the space and equipment, it is useful to keep a record of what needs changing for the future. In a small library, there may only be one exhibit case in the lobby, but if exhibits are to be used to encourage financial support and to enhance the library image, it could be important to look at the over-all physical space to see where expansion might be possible. Not only might the library add other exhibit cases, but it could also decide to use available wall spaces for upright displays or create some permanent area elsewhere, such as in a children's materials room, in a long corridor or even in a basement where book sales, meetings and social events are held.

In the best circumstances, display areas should be versatile, allowing for more than one exhibit case or stand, with a combination of wall and floor space. If the

Fig. 3.1. *(above)* Large open areas are usually suitable for exhibit space. Moveable cases on wheels help keep the space versatile.

Fig. 3.2. *(below)* This attractive open space in a main lobby area emphasizes browsing. A book exhibit here might complement this goal, suggesting reading topics to viewers.

library has storage facilities, such as a garage or bookmobile loading dock, moveable exhibit cases may be stored there when the exhibit area is needed for other purposes. Before purchasing new display cases, think through the materials preservation issues such as security and lighting. This is particularly important for exhibits that will have valuable or borrowed materials in them, as the library does not want to risk damage to materials that it cannot replace.

Library materials preservation considerations

Although a display's appearance is of primary importance to a successful exhibit, librarians should be aware that exhibited materials are at some physical risk. This may not be a pressing matter for replaceable items, books that are still in print and photocopied materials, but for any original pieces, it should be in the forefront of the exhibit coordinator's mind. Light, heat and air purity will quickly affect organic materials, and even plastics. Fading, buckling, mold and grime can all be serious hazards. The list below reviews the major issues:

Handling   Often overlooked, but extremely important are good handling techniques. Materials about to be exhibited should be examined carefully and if necessary, given treatment, encapsulation, repair or whatever is necessary to ready them for the exhibit. They should be treated carefully, not left unattended on open carts or stacked precariously on shelves while in process. The exhibit team should take the time to set out some guidelines as to where materials should be kept and, if necessary, train volunteers or student workers with little experience in basic handling techniques: how to shelve books with book ends, how to load a book truck safely, etc.

Conservation   Occasionally it is necessary to repair an item that is going on exhibit; books with detached title pages; fragile dust jackets, or texts out of their covers. It is tempting to just use tape or glue to get these items at least looking as though they are in one piece. In the end this will only add to the damage, so it is best to make repairs to conservation standards when they are first identified. Because books are constructed in many different ways, a single repair technique will not work for all. If your library does not have a conservation-trained repair technician, or for older, unusual and original materials, the exhibit team should look for a book conservator. The state historical society or university is a good place to start.

Lighting   While it is important to have good lighting for exhibits, it is more important to have safe lighting for your materials. When possible, it is best to have diffused light, that is, to make sure that lights are not trained directly on the materials themselves. All light damages library materials: the damage depends on the intensity of the light, the length of time the item is exposed and the kind of light to which it is exposed (ultraviolet is the big culprit here). Worse, the damage continues for a time even when the light source is

Fig. 3.3. *(above)* Materials waiting for exhibition should be shelved carefully in a secure, clean place to minimize handling damage.

Fig. 3.4. (below) Trucks should not be left with exhibit materials in disarray, with documents and fragile items at risk.

removed. So it follows that no materials, exhibited or not, should be exposed for any length of time to sunlight, any direct light, fluorescents that are not filtered for UV or any light that gives excessive heat.

Deflected light, such as that coming from windows covered by screening or vertical blinds will not carry significant UV, and UV filter sleeves are available to slip on over fluorescent tubes. UV filters are available for track lighting also, where they can simply be trained slightly to one side of the exhibit case rather than directly on the display. If you are not sure of lighting levels, borrow a light meter that reads UV levels: these should read from 50 to 100 lux maximum, the low end being most appropriate for vulnerable items such as letters, illustrations that may not be colorfast or fragile cloth. Turn off exhibition area lights when not needed.

Temperature and Humidity   These two elements affect one another. The warmer the air, the more humidity it can hold, so it follows that the ideal conditions are to keep a cool, relatively dry atmosphere inside the case. A general range is usually given as 45–55 percent relative humidity (Rh) and 65–75 degrees Fahrenheit (F). To avoid fading, curling, buckling and mold problems during the exhibit, the cases should be planned away from direct light that can cause heat and in a space that has good air circulation, preferably air conditioning.

Air circulation is important in combatting humidity problems. Large spaces usually do not have much trouble, but wall-mounted cases and other mounts against walls may be vulnerable because of diminished air circulation coupled with condensation due to fluctuating outside temperatures. Airless cul-de-sacs with high levels of dry heat in winter can be a problem as well. Try not to place exhibit cases near heating vents or radiators.

Mold is an insidious enemy of library materials. Usually, by the time you can actually see it with the naked eye, you are in trouble; spores spread rapidly. Humidity needs only to rise to above 68 percent with some accompanying heat, and within 48 hours, many molds may begin to grow. Few remedies are available to combat mold once you have it in the library. Even if every item is cleaned and shelves or spaces wiped down with Lysol or another mold inhibiting solution, as soon as the warm, humid conditions return, the mold will begin again. In choosing an exhibit space, pick a cool area that has as little humidity and heat fluctuation as possible.

To help maintain the most stable levels of Rh and temperature, silicone crystals may be placed in a aluminum pie pan or other such impermeable tray and put inside special comparments underneath cases, below the exhibit shelves or platform. Small cakes or squares of silicone can be used in a perforated covered tray right in the case itself.

Fig. 3.5. Silicone crystals are placed in a controlled atmosphere of 45–55 percent Rh to attain the desired humidity balance. Acclimatized trays of the crystals may be put inside exhibit cases to help control humidity fluctuation. If an exhibit case does not have a space below the inner platform, a cover such as the one on the right may be constructed, and the tray placed right in the exhibit case. Note the large space for air circulation in the cover. Silicone is also available in other forms such as cakes that sometimes come in pouches and are easier to use.

Monitoring Even when using silicone to help maintain stable conditions, a hygrothermograph or other devices that monitor the air for temperature and humidity are necessary. If the monitor shows that the air is becoming close to the top level of advisable humidity, it may be necessary to turn down the heat or even remove some valuable materials from the exhibit. Wet silicone trays must be replaced with dry ones. The wet trays may be dried out in a controlled atmosphere and used again.

Monitors come in every size and shape and price range, but do not buy the very cheap ones available in department stores. These will not retain their accuracy over time and usually cannot be recalibrated. Every library benefits from having one or two environmental monitors available for monitoring trouble spots, moldy basements or dry, hot areas. We have all seen the recording hygrotherographs in museums: these record continuously and the resulting graphs may be kept for historical records. But they are very expensive. For book exhibits, there are many smaller models that record both temperature and humidity, including some very small digital ones that are hardly noticeable in the cases.

Fig. 3.6. Left to right: Large plastic cased thermohygrometer, with a digital display for temperature at the bottom; two smaller and cheaper types that read both temperature and humidity, but have less accuracy than the larger one. At right, the top of the line, the recording hygrothermograph that records on a paper disk that can be retained for permanent records.

Permanent Display When new facilities are constructed in a library, often exhibit spaces are created with little thought as to exactly how they will be used. Glass-fronted spaces that are too low make it difficult or impossible to actually see the captions and materials. Often these are not used for exhibits, really, and are used for permanent storage or semi-exhibit (just some nice-looking items). Permanent exhibits of any kind are not advisable, no matter what the materials. Light will damage everything in time, and the weight of one book on another or the shape of a book stand can make a permanent indentation. Open books on permanent display must have the opening changed every few days to avoid damage from continued exposure to light. Well-framed documents behind UV-filtered glass are fairly well protected, but in general, a permanent exhibit is a bad idea.

Exhibit cases

When examining older exhibit cases and equipment, there are several very important requirements to think about. There should be no lighting or electrical fixtures inside, as this is a fire hazard and creates high levels of heat. Many older cases have interior lighting and must be used when there are no funds for replacing them, but under such circumstances, the exhibition period should be much shorter to avoid damage to the exhibited materials.

A flat exhibit case should incorporate some air space below the book platform for good air circulation, and in the best of all possible conditions, this space would be large enough to hold the tray of silicone moisture-absorbing crystals to keep high humidity in check. The display platform should not be permanently covered with a textile. While textiles may be used for visual effect, permanently installed textiles may become moldy or dirty over time. It is better to be able to change or remove the textile and store it in a clean place between exhibitions. The platform should be finished with an inert polyester-based varnish or paint that will not off-gas. When possible, the cases should be on wheels, to allow for multiple locations, but it is important to have a locking brake device to avoid unwanted movement. Security is an issue when considering types of exhibit cases: all should lock securely in some manner.

Many library supply houses offer simple exhibit cases for libraries, but it is best to list your own requirements for cases that will answer your libraries exhibit needs and then research widely on the subject before purchasing. Exhibition cases are expensive and getting just the right one can make all the difference in safety for your materials and ease of installation.

Here are four common types of exhibit cases a library might consider:

Flat cases   These can be square or oblong, usually with a high glass or Plexi-glas top and sides. The best can be beautiful to look at, with wooden bases of handsome materials. The disadvantage with these is that they take up considerable floor space and are best utilized in an area that allows viewing from three or four sides. In terms of the exhibit materials, flat cases are the best because items may be exhibited flat, or nearly so, as well as on book stands and supports. This flexibility means less installation effort and time on the part of the staff. The top may be lifted off using large rubber suction handles, or cases may be constructed with hand holds. Some flat cases open at one side and the platform pulls out.

Fig. 3.7. Flat cases in several styles: note that the large square one and the small rectangular one have high tops that can accommodate upright books, whereas the lower-sided case would require flat or only slightly raised exhibits.

Slanted-top cases   These are also quite good for display, but the slanted top means that viewing is mainly from the front, and sometimes, the slanted glass top is too low at the front edge to allow large books to be placed on upright stands or cradles. If the case is to be kept along a wall or back-to-back with another similar shaped case, this type may be preferred. In some cases, the slanted portion of the top opens to allow easy materials installation.

Upright cases   While upright cases are attractive with just the right materials in them, they limit the kinds of items that may be displayed. Some free-standing upright cases have several shelves, and may be approached from all sides.

But materials cannot be easily displayed in all directions at once, so the viewing pattern can be awkward. In addition, when lighting is from above, the top shelves cast shadows on the lower ones. Captions on lower shelves are harder to read, and large books often do not fit on the shelves when mounted in a book support stand. Flat display is fine for the middle shelf, but high shelves or the bottom ones are difficult to see. If all items are displayed flat on the shelves, the visual impact is lost to anyone not directly in front of the case.

Upright cases sometimes work well if they are wall-mounted. The back of the case can be used for posters or document display along with some books and artifacts on the shelves. But sometimes these have preservation problems, with poor air circulation and condensation. Older upright cases occasionally had fans mounted inside, theoretically for increased air circulation, but this proved to be problematical too, as unfiltered fans deposited particulate matter on the items on display. It is useful to have a few upright cases mixed in with most larger exhibits, but if the library will be using only one type of case, this is not a good selection.

Table-top or shelf-mounted cases   These may be especially useful to smaller libraries where spaces are limited and exhibits vary in size and type. These can be of several varieties: small upright glass cases with a shelf inside, or slanted-top or flat cases. They can even sometimes be made at home by an enterprising member of the library staff or friends group, or by a skilled cabinet maker.

Whether home-made or commercial, three main considerations are important in choosing a good exhibit case:

> **Air circulation must be adequate.** Air-tight cubes and boxes are often used in museums but when these are sealed, the air inside the case must be precisely right. For library exhibits, it is best to ensure good air circulation whenever possible.

> **Weight should be a consideration when estimating size.** The library will want cases to be portable, and since even small table cases can be fairly heavy, size and weight need to be considered before constructing or purchasing a case. A demountable table-top case, called the PolyCase, is constructed of clear acrylic panels, easy to store and available in many different shapes.

> **Quality of building materials.** Especially when making your own, keep in mind that plywood is almost universally treated with formaldehyde and other chemicals and will off-gas to the detriment of the exhibited materials. Untreated wood may be used, but then should be completely sealed with an inert polyurethane sealer. Do not use sealers that contain PVC or other chloride-based paints. Even with these precautions, books and documents should not lie directly on the wood. Plexiglas is most often used for in-house construction; plastics also must be made of inert acrylic or polyester.

Book and document supports

Just as important as the case itself, are the supports for the materials to be exhibited. Book supports and stands, documents enclosures, mounts for photographs and posters and in fact, everything that goes into the case with your exhibit materials should be carefully chosen. Many types of cardboard are highly acidic and should not be used for creating permanent book supports, not only because the acid content can transfer to the materials, but because highly acidic cardboard does not stand up over time and will need to be replaced often. The visual goal, when buying or creating book supports is to have them unobtrusive and neat, so that they do not distract from the item displayed or from the overall visual effect.

Fig. 3.8. A variety of book stands and an upright and two low types of Plexiglas stands.

Commercial book supports Book supports on the commercial market come in many forms, Some are wire wrapped in plastic, or metal folding stands. Some are molded or glued pieces of Plexiglas. Recently, large foam wedges have proved to be a versatile way of supporting books. In general, there are three criteria for a good book support:

1. The book support must cradle the book in such a way that the entire book is supported. It is important to make sure the book does not extend far enough off the support to cause sagging or warping while the book is on display. Especially the spine must be supported, since this is where the structural strength of the book resides, and when unsupported, spines may crack, sag or detach. Because books are so very different in size and shape, a single shape of book support usually does not work for all the items in an exhibit; rather it is a good idea to purchase or make several shapes and types of supports.

2. There should be no sharp edges that will come in contact with the book. In general, all surfaces should be smooth and rounded to avoid denting, cutting or slicing the pages or even the covers of books left for several months against them. Even smooth hard surfaces, where there is enough pressure, as in the case of a large, heavy book, can cause permanent dents.

3. The materials of which the stand is constructed, especially if the displayed item will rest directly on it, must be acid-free or alkaline if made of cardboard, and inert acrylic or polyester if a plastic material. If there is doubt, acid-free paper may cover the stand, or an unbleached, natural cotton cloth may be used. More on textiles below.

Foam wedges

Foam wedges have proved to be excellent for books that can lie open, spine down, since these wedges come in many sizes and shapes and are relatively inexpensive. But for books that need to be raised into an upright position, as is often the situation in a wall-mounted case, these wedges do not work because there is no lip to keep the book from sliding down the wedge.

Plexiglas, however, lends itself to this purpose: an upright support may be constructed and a lip attached at the bottom. Some, such as Benchmark Butterfly Book Mounts, combine metal and plastic materials in such a manner that the plastic cradles the book and the metal stand underneath allows adjustment of the support. Adjustable wire supports, whether they are covered or not are usually less satisfactory because there seem to be too many sharp edges, but occasionally these work for small, lightweight items. Many libraries purchase a number of the foam wedges and a variety of Plexiglas supports, and then rely on their own exhibit preparation staff to create the rest.

Fig. 3.9. Foam wedges used as book supports. The individual pieces make a variety of configurations possible. Note the spine support piece in the center.

Making your own

For libraries where major book exhibits are only an occasional thing, making all the supports for the materials may be appropriate. The danger is, however, in not making these carefully, and this will give an unprofessional or sloppy look to the whole exhibit. This can usually be avoided by copying a few simple diagrams in creating supports, and by using good, attractive materials in their construction. Specific material considerations include:

Supplies Many supplies for exhibition work can be found at a well-stocked art supply store. For libraries where exhibits are frequent enough, it will be cheaper to buy through a catalog such as those listed in the appendices. Here you will be able to find an acid-free card stock and museum board of an appropriate thicknesses, strong enough to hold books but thin enough to score and bend without cracking. Buy large sheets, because it is easier to have long strips to fold than to have to tape or glue pieces together. For small libraries, storing these large sheets is often a problem since they will sag and become unusable if stored on their sides. Supply storage will be discussed again below.

Avoid the temptation to buy colored paper and board stock for book stand construction. It is often hard to find acid-free colored stock, which must be color fast to be safe for the exhibit materials. Also, colored stock is more expensive, and in the end, the supports are often not really very visible. If color is desired on book supports, it is more effective to cover them with book cloth fabric, glued on.

Framing and encapsulating documents When buying museum board for framing documents and posters, color will be an important element in the overall visual effect. It is a good idea not to stock colored framing supplies unless you are sure they will be used up; instead, buy just the amount and color needed after the exhibit cases have been planned. Save all scraps, however: captions can often be mounted on these bits of colored board. If you decide to mat your own photographs or documents, a light tape will be required for hinging. Use a paper tape made for the purpose such as Filmoplast, found in catalogs that sell archival supplies such as Light Impressions or University Products. Never use masking or mailing tapes.

Another possibility for documents is encapsulation in clear plastic envelopes. It is an easy technique to learn and directions for the steps in making a Mylar envelope can be found in the appendices. The best part is that you can try it on a throw-away magazine cover first to perfect your skills. While there are precut Mylar envelopes commercially available, it is less expensive and more attractive to have them made in-house to fit the item exactly.

Two cautions concerning this technique: documents that have not been washed and deacidified should not be enclosed in an air-tight envelope in order to avoid creating a micro-environment that might aggravate acids already at work in the item. Instead, a three-sided envelope allowing some air circulation may by used, with most of the same

Fig. 3.10. Encapsulation is useful for many types of documents, large or small. These encapsulated manuscripts have been matted first to prevent the inks from actually touching the plastic.

advantages for exhibiting as the closed one. The other disadvantage is that the static cling created by the two plastic sheets may create harmful suction on documents that have raised inks, paints or seals on them, removing loose particles. These materials should not be encapsulated at all. But for most printed matter, encapsulation is fine.

Use a simple form When making your own book supports, it is essential to have a simple form that will not require a lot of ugly tape on the outside or show ragged edges. The forms should relate closely to the item being mounted; sometimes the book can be smaller or larger than the support, but this difference should not be very great. Some forms may be collapsed after use, and recut for another book next time.

Measure carefully Making your own book supports will be made easier by careful measuring. The preparator needs to know exactly at which page the book will be opened when on display. By opening the book in a natural fashion at this page, without forcing, it will be obvious at what angle the covers should lie. By placing a temporary support under the covers at that height, the height of the leg of the book support may be measured, and the distance from the leg to the spine as well. These, along with the width of the spine, are the crucial measurements.

Fig. 3.11. Measuring the height of the lift of the cover before making the book support.

Fig. 3.12. An elegant, cloth-covered and raised book support, matched to the background of the exhibit case. (Courtesy of the Huntington Library, San Marino, CA.)

The problems of taping   Taping the book support form is possible, sometimes necessary and fast, but if the exhibit is likely to be in a too damp or too dry situation, tape will often peel off. The best result is obtained by using strips of non-adhesive book cloth of the type used in book repair, which are glued in place. This does not take very long if strips are precut. If a self-adhesive tape must be used, the clear type used on paperback spines, available from library supply houses, is much preferable to heavy self-adhesive tapes like strapping tape or plastic tape that can ooze adhesive under warm conditions. Transparent tape of the type used for office work is not strong enough.

Four basic designs: You will see that the diagrams for folded book supports have several versatile features.

The Cradle Design   It can be scored and folded so as to support a book opened in the middle, or with the opening at the right or left, simply by folding the leg of the cradle to be higher or lower. In addition, the form may be flattened out again for easy storage. Scoring at the fold points should be done with a few light strokes of a mat knife, so as to cut into the cardboard about half way or less. Some cuts must be made neatly on the right side of the board, but some will need to be made on the opposite side (dotted lines). Textiles may be draped over the cradle, and if a library is lucky enough to have a good craftsperson who knows how to manipulate cloth well, a book cloth covering may be glued to the board. But this last requires significant handwork, labor and time. The book is then tied to the support at the desired opening with thin clear plastic tape.

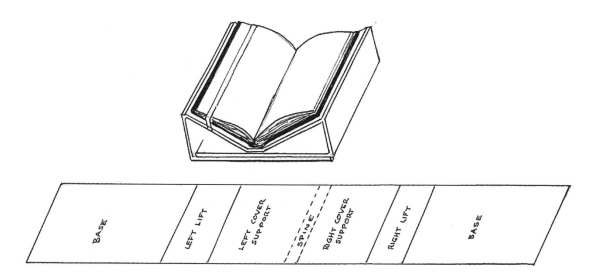

Fig. 3.13. The Cradle Design: A folding book support with a double base. The bases are attached with double-sided self-adhesive tape of the type used in making encapsulation envelopes.

The Upright Design Because many libraries have only standing cases, it is essential to have a basic upright support design. The standing support can be manipulated similarly to the cradle: By increasing the height of the support and back, and widening and slanting the lip, the stand can accommodate bigger books. By manipulating the back support, the stand can be made to sit less upright and recline more. Both of these designs are secured after folding with glued strips of book cloth or cloth tape. This tape may simply be peeled off if flat storage is desired later. The lip of the stand must be deeper than the depth of the book being displayed to prevent sagging of the cover or text. Again, the book must be secured by tying it to the support.

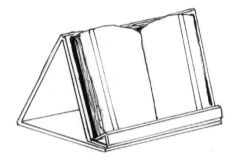

Fig. 3.14. The Upright Support: The lip rests on the front of the base. Dotted lines indicate that scoring and cuts must be made on the opposite side of the board from the other cuts. The lip support may be glued, but will be weak if not also taped or covered with book cloth.

BASE	BACK SUPPORT	FRONT SUPPORT	LIP BASE	OUTSIDE LIP	INSIDE LIP

The Flat Support This is done in the same manner as the other folded supports, to provide a firm surface for a cover that will lie open fully.

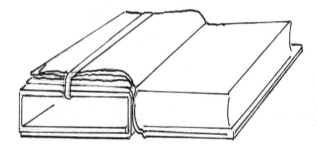

Fig. 3.15. The Flat Support: A simple folded support, with a double base.

The Book Futon Invented at the Newberry Library in Chicago for holding vulnerable books that patrons needed to consult, this fabric support can be attractive. While it is not available commercially and it takes a bit of skill to sew one, it is inexpensive, easy to use and store, and it offers the possibility of colorful backgrounds for exhibition materials. The ends are simply rolled under and secured with Velcro, and the book laid gently on the thick futon, the rolled ends acting as support for the covers. There are two rolled positions to create higher and lower cover angles.

The fabric must be just the right thickness: not too thick to sew, not so thin that it is floppy or weak. A mid-weight to light-weight, tightly woven cloth is best. It is imperative that the cloth be color-fast, and the Velcro pieces should match as much as possible in order not to show very much on the finished product. Below is a diagram of both sides of a book futon.

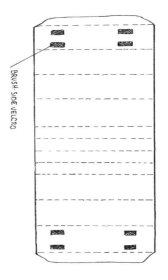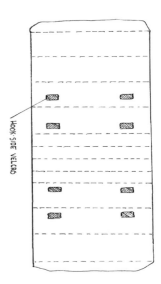

Fig. 3.16. The Book Futon Diagram: Dotted lines indicate sewing. Futon must be stuffed with the quilting bat before sewing, and this makes it imperative that the sewing stitch be quite long. Nylon or other strong thread is best. Velcro squares are sewn on at the end. Materials needed: Thin, but tightly woven cloth, medium weight; eight pairs of Velcro squares; medium quilting batt with a minimum of 1" loft; thread to match. Small size: 28" x $11^1/_2$"; large size: 35" x 18" (needs larger pieces of Velcro).

Other supports and for small exhibits and displays Here again, tips for many good constructions may be found in *The Library Display Handbook*. Preparators should remember, however, that stands made out of old acid, cardboard boxes and wire are not appropriate for many original, fragile or valuable library materials, or for books and documents that are on display for several months at a time. Dust jackets will often be compromised after being pinned tightly to an acid board; stands made out of coat hangers may hold a book well enough but leave permanent indentations in the dust jacket or cover resting on them. Items included in wall displays will sag easily, those clipped with bulldog clips will retain the clip marks forever afterwards. So, while it is desirable to have the ability to make supports of all kinds in-house, in planning exhibits, the quality of the support materials should be included in the decision-making process.

Fig. 3.17. The Book Futon is rolled at each side to support the covers of the books, and secured by the means of the Velcro strips.

Mounting and installing the materials

A month or so before the exhibit is to be installed, when all the materials are chosen for the exhibit, they should be examined closely to see if any need repair and to measure for the various sorts of stands and mounts that will be necessary. When installation starts, there is still some preparation:

Cleaning   Materials should be cleaned a day or so before the exhibit is installed, away from the exhibit area and other books. For cleaning, a large, very soft bristle brush and a clean, lint-free cotton cloth are best. Clean the exhibit area in general first (vacuuming, mopping, general dusting). Do not allow the use of spray cleaners as the residue can end up on your exhibit cases and shelves, eventually getting on the books. The person mounting the exhibit should clean inside the cases and shelving **as they are installing the exhibit,** so that the minimum of particulate matter is enclosed with the exhibit materials. A dry cotton cloth may be used, but there are several treated dust cloths that are safe that pick up dust and do not release it. One Wipe dust cloths can often be found in local supermarkets, and Stretch 'N Dust, a Chicopee shop cloth, is also safe for this purpose. It is not recommended to use these cloths directly on the books and materials themselves, however.

Fig. 3.18. Notice the extra-wide strip of Mylar holding the weight of this book's cover safely, without allowing the pages to flop over.

Tying books safely   In general, unless a book already falls open easily, it is better not to exhibit it entirely flat. Since many books do not have the type of spine that is intended for such wide opening, the sewing or structure of the book will be compromised by tying them or forcing them open to this degree over the period of the exhibit. Even when a book lies open easily, the covers usually need support. Sometimes, a book will lie open easily in a book cradle and not require tying. But often, humidity changes will curl or buckle pages that are not secured. Tying with $^3/_4$" Mylar clear film or other polyester or polypropylene tape is recommended. This tape, when used carefully, is safe for tying even fragile items. It is placed over the open page and around the support firmly, but not tightly, and secured underneath by taping the two ends together with $^1/_4$" double-sided, self-adhesive tape or another narrow, clear tape in a manner so that the adhesive tape does not touch the book itself. Reading or viewing the text is not impeded by the clear plastic strip.

     There is a rolled string of plastic also available for the same purpose, but it has sometimes indented the paper of exhibit items when pulled too tightly. The flat tape seems easier to use safely.

Documents   Flat items such as maps, letters and other documents can often be displayed just as they are. But they too are sometimes affected by humidity changes or strong lighting: photographs will begin to curl or fade, paper will buckle. For especially fragile materials there are several choices:

Photocopying allows some materials to be on exhibit that would otherwise be damaged by display for long periods or by travel. This is a particularly useful tool for displaying photographs. Be sure that a person trained in preservation photocopying does the work, however, if there is any doubt about the vulnerability of the item during this process.

Encapsulation, as described above, offers still another safe method of display. This technique of enclosing a document in two sheets of Mylar inert plastic leaves the item safe from dirt, dust and poor handling.

Clear glass weight: For some documents that are not vulnerable to weight, such as those with raised inks or seals, clear glass or Plexiglas weights such as have been described later in the chapter for use with captions, can be used. This is a fast way of making your documents look nice.

Exhibit design and ambience

Almost as important as the exhibit items themselves are the surroundings of the exhibit materials. No matter how wonderful the materials or how important the information, if the result is not visually stimulating, the exhibit will be passed over, only glanced at or completely ignored by most passersby. This is where every exhibit coordinator must put their imagination, and their color sense to work. Colorful textiles, artifacts that relate to the theme, flags, posters, maps, cutouts, videos, and more can make the difference to the over-all design.

There needs to be not only an over-all design, including placement of cases, any standing displays or furniture, but individual, internal case designs as well. Each case must have its own visual integrity, neither too crowed nor too empty. Every exhibit needs a central visual note: look at every exhibit as if you were a viewer. On entering the exhibit area, what is the first thing that takes your eye? If it is a major part of the exhibit, a poster or the colorful part of the intended display, fine. If your eye goes on down the corridor or sees an unrelated piece of furniture first, you are not doing so well.

Here are a few tips for case design: Some of the same rules for the design of publications in the next chapter apply very well when designing a case: focus, balance and unity. Try not to design all your exhibit cases in the same way each time. If you have used brightly colored textiles in the first exhibit, try something else for visual effect next time. Vary your props and color schemes to get a fresh, new look. If all of your exhibit pieces are small, think of some large props to offset a busy feeling, with the opposite tech-

nique for many large pieces. Have the exhibit team look over the cases once they are actually in and comment on the visual impact: if you are installing a day or two in advance of any event such as an opening reception, you have time to change some of the background and props.

Textiles: Using textiles is not as simple as it may sound. While they offer wonderful possibilities for color excitement, many materials are not easy to use. Slippery fabric, unless used in a flat case is hard to handle. It is important not to use cheap, heavily dyed and chemically treated fabrics that will off-gas inside a closed case over the exhibit period, since such gasses can affect the organic substances of the books and documents. Pure materials such as cotton, unbleached muslin, wool, velvet are usually fine. If a cloth actually touches the books, make sure you have color fast and stable dyes, so that no color will transfer to the item being exhibited. When used with valuable library materials, it is best to test cloth for a few weeks to

Fig. 3.19. A well-designed case for a large variety of different objects offers focus and visual interest. (Courtesy of Memorial Library, Madison, WI.)

see if there is any dye loss or acid transfer when plain paper is pressed against it or when it is dipped in water. Often, fabric can be used effectively for covering the table platform, or hung at the back of a case where no materials actually touch it. Velveteen, for example, gives a rich, luxurious background for older materials.

Labeling and Captions: Here is another area where neatness and attention to visual matters make a lot of difference. Captions should be included in the case design. In an exhibit case where the books and objects may look just right, the introduction of many long captions can spoil the effect and produce a crowded appearance. Sometimes two or more related books may be included in the same caption, for example in an exhibit where two different editions of the same book are displayed for comparison. Colored backgrounds or borders may be used to good effect with captions where the other objects in the case are fairly dull looking.

It is easy to overlook the importance of the way captions look. Here are a few tips on making good looking ones:

1. Produce captions on a typewriter or computer with an attractive typeface. Cut these up on a paper cutter or with a ruler and mat knife (never with scissors), leaving at least an inch all the way around the text, more if you like the looks of wide margins. Avoid the temptation to justify the right-hand margin since readability will be sacrificed when words must be hyphenated or spaced unevenly. The paper should be good quality bond, white, off-white or some light shade that shows up the type well.

2. Mount this paper on small pieces of cardboard or foam core. This can be done with double-sided tape, glue stick, adhesive spray (keep this away from everything else!) or white glue. The board may be colored mat board, cut $1/8$" or more larger than the caption to make a colored border. Or, before mounting, a colored ink border may be drawn on the caption around the text for a neat, crisp look.

3. If mounting captions seems like too much work, a quick and attractive solution is to have

Fig. 3.20. A case of basically dull-looking books is given excitement and movement by a large caption and an effective background of a blown-up illustration.

Fig. 3.21. Here a diagram of the objects in the case is a key to a large caption placed to one side in a mini-exhibit where space is limited.

various sizes of plexiglass cut and sanded to smooth the edges, then cut the captions to match. The paper caption is simply laid on the exhibit case and the Plexiglas placed exactly on top.

4.   In the event of too little caption space in the cases, here is a way of avoiding individual captions. All the information may be placed on a large, major caption with a key of numbers—either a drawing of numbered items or by placing the numbers in the case next to each item. These are harder for the viewer to use, but sometimes necessary in cases where space is at a premium.

Fig. 3.22. In another method of saving caption space, items are numbered to refer to the single, central caption in the background.

Posters and Large Size Labels: Another important aspect of exhibition labeling is the manner in which the purpose and major themes are posted. A poster is always a good idea, if at all possible. It can combine the exhibit title and subtitles with an image, where desired. One of these should be among the first thing that catches the eye in most exhibits. Finances may only allow one or two: smaller announcement posters can be made on computer, or by hand using the many aids that can be found in art supply stores. A poster that is too small will simply not be noticed, so make them big enough for the space in which they will be displayed. Some good ideas and tips are in the next chapter on promotional materials.

Exhibits of more than three or four cases also need to have some large lettered theme announcements to guide the viewer from point to point. Though most theme labels are placed inside the case, as a change, self-adhesive letters (and even numbers, if the exhibit has a particular order of progression) in a bright color or black may be used to good effect right on the outside of the glass. Theme identification helps the viewer to quickly recognize the materials in each case. Usually, such labels do not take the place of captions.

Supplies and suppliers

It is tempting to buy exhibit supplies a bit at a time as you need them, and this approach is probably correct for smaller libraries that do not have exhibits very often or do not have storage space and more than one or two exhibit cases. But in general, this is an expensive way to put together appropriate exhibit supplies. Certain basic materials for mounting an exhibit can be found in local art supply stores, and textiles can often be bought in the major sewing outlet in your area, but acid-free board, monitoring devices, lettering, poster materials can often be purchased more economically through catalogs or firms that specialize in such things. Collect a few catalogs of this type (listed in the appendices) and become familiar with their offerings. Call in orders when possible because it is often possible to establish a contact who can be of help when you aren't sure exactly what you need. When specialty firms don't want to sell small amounts of papers and board, consider sharing a larger amount with the local school or another library such as the local historical society.

Storing supplies is often a problem at smaller libraries. Most libraries have a work area where repairs may be made to their books, supplies can be unpacked and packages wrapped, in short, a staging area. This is the appropriate place to add exhibit preparation. For libraries that do not have such a workstation, the appendices include a diagram for a simple construction that will serve for all of these purposes, with under-bench storage for large sheets of board and paper that are needed in good quality book repair as well as in exhibit work. Even if a small area, a few deep shelves are useful to house the awkward shapes of book supports, large pieces of fabric, etc. It is a good idea to save all the trappings of a really good, basic book exhibit. The same exhibit, or one that uses some of the same materials may come in handy later, to fill in when funds for developing an entirely new exhibit are low.

Publicity and Promotion

Chapter Four

Jane Pearlmutter

Promotion and publicity materials will be an important part of the planning for your exhibit. Not only do you want to make sure that people come to see it, your publicity should help to increase the library's visibility and support from its community.

These days we are bombarded by print materials. Desktop publishing has made graphic design accessible, but not everyone sitting at the computer is a designer. This chapter will address the principles and methods of graphic design along with a look at other publicity methods. If you are a talented artist and/or trained designer you can break all the rules! But if you are new to graphic design, following basic design guidelines will help you avoid the homemade look.

Although there is an abundance of poorly designed material out there, there is also much that is beautiful and sophisticated. Those who see our publicity materials are also exposed to high quality design and printing and now expect something more attractive and visually exciting—the typed and mimeographed piece will no longer catch the eye! Your print materials are lasting, physical representations of your library and its services. Impressions are important, and the look and tone of your publications conveys an image.

Before you start the writing or design of any piece, you should know the answers to the following questions: Why are you printing the piece? What is the purpose of the publication? Why is it needed? What kind of image do you want to project? Does it need to conform to a template or larger institutional style? Whom do you want to read it? Do you know the audience? What kind of information will it include?

When is it needed? Is it a dated publication? Who should review it before printing? How will it be distributed? Will the distribution method affect the format? How many will be needed? What is the budget? How will it be reproduced? What kinds of art will be needed? What resources are available?

Most of us have had little training for the role of designer of print materials. Perhaps your boss now assumes that because there is a computer and laser printer in your office, all publicity materials can now be created in house. Perhaps you are intrigued by the capabilities of your computer and are anxious to learn new skills and computer programs. Or possibly you only have access to word processing but have no budget for outside design help. In any case, you can create professional-looking materials that catch the eye and enhance the image of the library.

Types of printed materials

When choosing the types of printed pieces that will best publicize your exhibit, the answers to the above questions will help you decide. If you have or can obtain a good mailing list, and have the budget for postage, a self-mailer brochure or flyer may be the most efficient way to reach your audience. If your library already publishes a monthly calendar or newsletter, an insert into that publication, or a "display ad" in that piece may be the most efficient way to get the word out. If you would primarily like to alert people who may be visiting the library anyway, bookmarks, flyers at the circulation desk, and eye-catching posters (at least 11" x 17") will be important.

The most important thing to remember when planning the design of a printed piece is that your primary purpose is communication. There is information in that piece that you must convey, and the design is part of that communication, rather than just decoration. The message of the piece is a factor in determining the look of the piece. All the design elements—type, flow, graphics, white space, paper and ink—should be chosen to enhance readability and increase communication. But it's also important to remember that the reader is a viewer first: there must be something to grab the attention.

Basic design guidelines

These basic elements give publications a coherent look.

Focus   Create a focus for the page with large, bold display type or graphics. Contrast elements with size density and position.

Balance   Weight elements in terms of size, position, interest. Don't overcrowd type and graphics. Group the white (empty) space.

Flow   Create directional flow on the page with lines, type, and paths of white space. Consider the "Z" pattern of reading when placing information (the eye usually moves from top left to top right, then to bottom left and bottom right).

Unity   Use consistent type and graphic motifs. Use restraint with spot color and typefaces. Use a grid to place elements on a page.

Fig. 4.1. Display type and a large graphic give this flyer/poster focus, balance, flow and unity.

Creating a grid

The grid is an arbitrary division of the page into rectangles. It is your blue-print for the design of a publication. With a grid, all pages in your publication will have a consistent look and one page or panel will flow into the next. The grid may consist of a few large rectangles, such as dividing a page into three columns, or it may have many small elements. The content will determine the appropriate grid. All elements that are placed on the page fit a unit or combination of units of the grid, and the rest of the space is left white.

Take the time to come up with a workable grid. You will be able to use it over and over. If you do a regular publication, such as a newsletter, use the same grid each time. Brochures, posters, and other "one-time" pieces can be laid out on new grids. Page layout programs and some word processing pro-grams make it extremely easy to create a grid. Specify the size of the margins, the number of columns and space between them, pull down a few horizontal guidelines and you have an instant grid. If you are doing your layout manu-ally, mark the grid on graph paper or layout boards.

The grid is, of course, invisible in your finished product. All elements— type, photos, charts, boxes, border—usually touch these invisible grid lines on at least two sides. The elements may cover several units of the grid. But not all areas of the grid will be filled in.

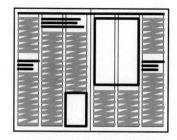
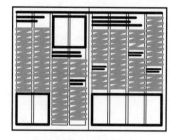
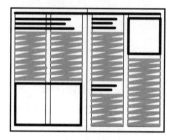

Fig. 4.2. Sample grids with two-, three- and four-column formats.

Columns

Column widths must be chosen with the content of the piece in mind. News-letters with a great deal of text are generally more readable in two or three columns. Narrower columns, which can have smaller type, are suitable for lists or short items. If a column of text requires frequent hyphenation, it is probably too narrow. On the other hand, lines longer than 65 characters are harder to read.

White space

White space isn't necessarily white. It is the empty space on the page, and it will be whatever color paper your piece is printed on. Inexperienced design-ers often fear the empty space and look for graphic elements to fill it up. But white space is a necessary part of the page. It gives the eye a place to rest and keeps your design from looking too cluttered. Framing important informa-tion or an illustration in white space makes it stand out clearly and gives it more weight. Even when you have too much information for the size of your publication, work on editing your text rather than eliminating white space.

How does empty space add such visual impact to a page? Think of the empty space inside a gothic cathedral. Is that soaring ceiling a waste of space or a beautiful architectural element? The white space must be grouped together to have this impact. If it is scattered around the page or trapped between columns it may look like something was left off the page.

Using type

The right typeface sets the style and tone of your piece. It should be chosen to enhance readability, and though it is often beautiful and decorative it should not overwhelm the text. Typefaces can be serious, casual, traditional, modern, elegant, fun, silly, and your choice will convey a certain image.

Restrict the number of typefaces in a single publication. One or two should suffice. Combine typefaces carefully, avoiding combinations that are too similar. For greatest contrast, use sans serif faces for display and serif faces for body text; for less contrast use the same typeface in different sizes and weights. (Serif typefaces are those with the little "tails" on the end of the letters; they are generally considered more readable than sans serif typefaces).

The
Type
You
Choose
Creates
A
Mood

THE
TYPE
YOU
CHOOSE
CREATES
A
MOOD

Sample Head in San Serif Type

Body text is easier to read in a serif typeface. In this case the font is a standard Times Roman. The size is 10 point. Because of the narrow column the text is set left aligned. Not all types are equally easy to read. Setting type in all caps or italics also makes it harder to read when used for longer passages.

Sample Head in Serif Type

Body text is easier to read in a serif typeface. In this case the font is a standard Times Roman. The size is 10 point. Because of the narrow column the text is set left aligned. Not all types are equally easy to read. Setting type in all caps or italics also makes it harder to read when used for longer passages.

Sample Head in San Serif Type

BODY TEXT IS EASIER TO READ IN A SERIF TYPEFACE. IN THIS CASE THE FONT IS LYTHOS. THE SIZE IS 10 POINT. BECAUSE OF THE NARROW COLUMN THE TEXT IS SET LEFT ALIGNED. NOT ALL TYPES ARE EQUALLY EASY TO READ. SETTING TYPE IN ALL CAPS OR ITALICS ALSO MAKES IT HARDER TO READ WHEN USED FOR LONGER PAS-SAGES.

Sample Head in Serif Type

Body text is easier to read in a serif typeface. In this case the font is a standard Times Roman Italic. The size is 10 point. Because of the narrow column the text is set left aligned. Not all types are equally easy to read. Setting type in all caps or italics also makes it harder to read when used for longer passages.

Change the font style (same typeface, different size, weight or style) **for functional distinctions between different types of information and** *for emphasis.*

Limit the use of all capital letters, boldface, and italics to small blocks. Do not use decorative or script typefaces as body text.

Balance the size of headlines to body text. Don't overpower the text.

Choose a size that is easily readable. Do not set body text smaller than 10 points.

Keep line length under 65 characters. Do not use justified type for narrow columns. Watch for rivers of white space in justified blocks of type. Do not center type except for posters or invitations.

Graphics

A graphic element will add interest to your publication. This might include decorative borders, boxes, shaded areas, and your logo as well as the more obvious choices of artwork or photos. If there is an item in your exhibit than can be reproduced on your printed materials that would be the logical choice. Permission to reproduce may be necessary.

If a number of illustrations are used in a piece, they should all have the same style. Your library's logo should also be present somewhere on every piece, but it may be kept small. Do not try to put in too many graphic elements or the piece will look cluttered.

High quality clip art (copyright free) is available in several formats—in books, on disk, or on compact disks. The clip art available on CD-ROM has grown tremendously in the last couple of years, and is quite inexpensive. If you use clip art from a book and want to add it to a computer-generated layout, you can either scan it in and print it with your page, or simply paste it in to the finished page.

If you are using photographs, indicate space in your layout by leaving a "keyline"—an open boxed area in the desired size. Label each photo to indicate where it goes in the layout. You may also prefer to have halftones made of your photos and then trim and place them yourself.

Layout methods

The final piece you give your printer is called the pasteup (also known as mechanicals or boards). Pasteup tools have changed considerably since the introduction of desktop publishing. If you are using a dtp program, you may not have to do any other layout work since all items are already positioned on the page. You still need to provide a printed copy of your piece to the printer.

For a manual layout, you will need to use an adhesive that will allow repositioning. Spray adhesives, wax (either from a table or hand-held waxer or a wax stick), and rubber cement are some of the choices. Apply the adhesive to the back of your page or pieces to be pasted in and position them on the pasteup grid (you can buy layout board with the grid marks on them). Tape a piece of tissue paper to the top of your board. Not only will this protect your pages, the tissue overlays carry the instructions to the printer. Mark the instructions (i.e. photo position, color, screening). Write your name and phone number on the pasteup boards below the grid lines.

Paper and ink selections

Discuss your ink and paper options with your printer as you plan your piece. For environmental reasons you may want to ask for recycled paper and soy-based inks. When using colored ink and colored paper, request a sample if possible to check the combination. One color printing is the least expensive, but any color can be printed in tones or lighter shades of the original color. Screens and percentage tints can appear to add additional colors.

Choose a paper with good opacity, especially if you are printing on both sides. If the piece is to be a self-mailer, you will need a more substantial weight of paper. If cost is a consideration, keep your publication to a standard size of paper.

Printing

Getting a print estimate

To provide an estimate for a printing job, the printer will need the following information:

The dimensions of the piece: 8.5X11 and 11X17 are standard sizes, and will provide you will a more economical quote than a special trim size.

The number of colors: For most printing work this will range from black, which you should state on the request, to 4-color work. If printing color, you have a choice of process color (color created by a process blend of four basic colors, as used in color photographs) or spot color (in which case you will select can choose very specific colors from a PMS chart book).

The type of paper: Weight, bulk, size, acidity, opacity, color and design choices are all very numerous. Printers will have in-house papers which are usually less expensive to use and are available immediately. If you select a paper not in the printers house stock it will need to be ordered and this may add to your timeline. You should be sure to ask.

The quantity to be printed: Quantity is an important factor in choosing the printer you use as this will most often affect the quote. Printers have equipment that is designed to print efficiently in certain quantity ranges, and you will quickly be able to identify which printers are best able to handle the kind of pieces you need to produce, as their quotes will be significantly lower that others.

Any special needs such as preparation of photographs, scoring or folding, inserts. Send a sample, clearly marked with exactly what you need whenever possible.

The type of printer you select will be based on the number of copies needed and the dimensions of your piece.

You will want to get in touch with your printer long before the piece is ready to go to press. Your printer is an excellent source of advice. They can offer design suggestions, paper swatches, suggest formats that will work best with their equipment, and can find ways to save you money. If you're unfamiliar with the printing process, ask lots of questions, especially about how they want materials prepared.

Always order a proof with any printing job. Check the type for broken or missing characters, check page numbers for order, make sure margins are straight and photos are in the right place with the right captions. This is not the time to change copy or look for spelling errors (though they can be corrected)—that should have been taken care of with thorough proofreading at the prepress stage.

Types of Printers

	Laser Printout	Photocopies	Quick Copy Printing	Metal Plate Offset
Number of copies	Less than 10	Less than 100	100–5,000	More than 5,000
Size	Usually 8.5X11	8.5X11 to 11X17	Usually up to 11X20	Large and non-standard sizes
Special abilities	Can also do transparencies	Collating, double-sided copies	Photos, paper variety, some color	Spot color, full color, bleeds, photos, screens, etc.
Preparation of originals	If printout will be used for doing a pasteup, use a wax holdout paper. 300 dpi laser output is adequate for photocopying or quick printing	limit large black areas, reverse type; photocopies tend to fade out	Consult with print shop. 8.5 x 11 original from laser printer is generally adequate; mechanical needed for some jobs	Prepare mechanical on boards with registration marks, crop marks, and overlays as needed. Output from at least 600 dpi printer. Consult with printer about requirements; may possibly supply everything on disk

Distribution

If your printed piece is designed to be mailed, check with the post office before you prepare the piece. The U.S. Postal Service can send you information about size requirements, postal regulations, and discounts for presorted mailings. Work backwards from the date that you want the piece in someone's hand. For a local audience, two weeks before the opening of your exhibit should be sufficient. If you are inviting people to an opening reception, that should have a little more lead time. Allow enough time for printing and mail delivery, particularly if you are mailing at bulk rate which can be considerably slower than first class mail.

Reinforce your mailed piece with posters in the library and flyers or bookmarks at the circulation desk. Printed additional copies of brochures to stock literature racks at the library and other public places. Think about your audience for this exhibit and where you are most likely to reach them.

Fig. 4.3. Postcards can serve as both exhibit announcements and invitations to a reception. (Courtesy of the Lexington (KY) Public Library.)

Other methods of publicizing your exhibit

Know your local media.

Keep a media list for your community. Include the daily and weekly newspapers, television and radio stations, specialty publications (such as newsletters from church or community groups) directed at particular segments of the community, and newspapers and radio stations operated by schools and colleges. Get to know who covers library, education, arts and related issues. Keep track of their deadlines, so you can provide information well in advance.

Send a press release.

The press release should be in narrative form. It should contain the five W's (Who, What, When, Where, and Why) and How. Put the most important information in the first paragraph and aim to grab the reader's attention with the first statement.

Reporters are always looking for good story ideas. Provide background information that will tie your exhibit to a larger subject. Include a short, interesting quote by the third paragraph.

Indicate when news organizations are free to use the information in the release. You may use FOR IMMEDIATE RELEASE, or specify a date. Use your organization's letterhead. Indicate one person to contact for information, with a phone number (be sure this is a number that is always answered or has an answering machine or voice mail).

Write a public service announcement.

Radio stations must include a certain number of public service announcements (psa) in their programming. Similar to your press release, it should be written to be read aloud in 30 seconds or less. Television stations are unlikely to use announcements that are not on video, but may announce your exhibit in a community calendar feature. Your cable company or public access station may also run a calendar of events that does not require video footage.

Write articles for non-library publications.

A state magazine or chamber of commerce publication might be interested in an article on a subject that is tied to your exhibit. Check first for the appropriate length and deadline.

For more detailed information on design principles and production of publications, the following books are excellent sources:

Adler, Elizabeth W. *Everyone's Guide to Successful Publications.* Berkeley, CA: Peachpit Press, 1993.

Williams, Robin. *The Non-Designer's Design Book.* Berkeley, CA: Peachpit Press, 1994.

Borrowing and Renting or Loaning an Exhibit

Chapter Five

Traveling exhibits offer a special variety of exhibits for libraries. Here, a discussion of how to find and plan for them, with some examples of costs and space requirements for exhibits offered by national institutions, also looks at the possibility of borrowing or loaning more local exhibits. A form for borrowing or lending agreements and a questionnaire for pre-exhibit information can be photocopied and adapted to precisely fit the needs of your library.

Traveling exhibits

Traveling exhibits offer an excellent alternative to or combination with those created in-house. Exhibits are available through such programs as those at the Library of Congress Interpretive Programs Office, from the American Library Association and the Texas Humanities Resource Center. In looking for a traveling exhibit, the initial step is to research the subjects available, costs and the space and security requirements to find one that will suit your library. These publications can help:

> *The Whole Person Catalog: The Source for Information About Arts and Humanities Programming in Libraries*, published by Public Programs, American Library Association, 50 East Huron St., Chicago, Ill 60611.
>
> > This catalog contains a section entirely on traveling exhibits, complete with information on subject, size, cost and contact people.

> *Guide to Traveling Exhibition Organizers*, 1994 edition, edited by Shirley Reiff Howarth, Humanities Exchange, Inc., P.O. Box 1608, Largo, FL 34649.
>
> > This publication lists a large number of traveling exhibitions in the U.S. The Humanities Exchange offers a newsletter on current traveling exhibitions with membership.

Planning

As with planning for in-house exhibits, there are a number of considerations that are paramount in choosing a traveling exhibit. Remember that these exhibits are often booked up far ahead: look into availability at least a year ahead of the date you want to have them in your library.

Space: The size of the library exhibit area will dictate how large an exhibit to sign up for. A nice exhibit can become unattractive if too crowded, or some items may be damaged if there is not enough space. However, some traveling exhibits are versatile in design; they can sometimes be set up down a long but wide corridor, for example.

Security: Traveling exhibitions have a wide range of security requirements. Many, usually panel or poster shows, require minimal security, but others include original materials where a high level of security is necessary. If you decide to rent or borrow an exhibit, it will come with instructions on installation, time frames for receipt and return, security and insurance forms. This does not release your library from the responsibility of having its own internal framework for exhibit schedules, permission and insurance/liability forms and at least minimal security. Many shows will not be available to the library which does not have these in place.

Publicity: While some exhibits have complete promotional materials available to publicize the exhibit, your library may need additional publicity avenues such as local newspaper, radio and TV announcements, and events planned to complement the exhibit. Organizations such as the American Library Association (ALA) have vigorous lecture, film and book programs as well, often attached to the exhibit.

Costs: Such exhibits vary widely in the expense entailed. Some beautifully produced exhibitions carry a $1,000 fee or more up front, while others have fees less than $200 or none at all. It should be taken into consideration at the outset that even when charges are nominal, that some expenditures fall to the host library; it is sometimes necessary to pay the travel and of course any installation costs once the materials are in your library, as well as packing and shipping afterward.

EVEN WHEN TRAVELING EXHIBIT FEES ARE NOMINAL, SOME EXPENDITURE OFTEN FALLS TO THE HOST LIBRARY

Two examples of traveling exhibits

The Bonfire of Liberties

In 1994, a traveling exhibit *The Bonfire of Liberties*, produced by the Texas Center for the Book and sponsored by the Library of Congress Center for the Book in Washington, became available through any state Center for the Book, which in turn looked for a host site in their state. Each state could have the exhibit up to four months, so ideally, it would go to more than one site in a state.

The exhibit arrived in four specially built crates, with a total weight of 600 lbs. Each state Center for the Book was responsible for costs and insurance for approximately $5,000 value when shipping to the next state on a date predetermined by the Library of Congress Center for the Book which handled all scheduling. In a case where a state Center for the Book could not afford these costs, the Library of Congress Center for the Book would negotiate financial assistance.

Each participating state was expected to designate a coordinator. The space requirement was 42 feet if all the panels were mounted on the wall. If the panels were free-standing, 25' x 1$\frac{1}{2}$' were required. Accompanying brochures were free to all participants. Camera-ready artwork was available for copying for posters and bookmarks, etc. Most state centers provided the host sites with flyers and handled publicity in the form of press releases and posters. In some cases, the host sites provided accompanying events, receptions and lectures. Consequently, costs were usually, in effect, shared by the Library of Congress Center for the Book, the Texas Center for the Book, and the host site institutions.

The exhibit itself consisted of eighteen framed panels of photographs, drawings and texts, on mats behind Plexiglas in brown frames. They could be displayed on free-standing legs or mounted on the wall. A small bookcase was included to house once-censored or "challenged" books which would require a table or stand at the host site.

The panels included subject matter that covered censorship through the ages, all forms of censorship, the motives behind censorship, rights of the reader and defense of a free press, specific censorship—in religion, philosophy, drama and theater, children's books, art, biography, history, and literature. The panels contained portraits of well known writers, documents and pages from censored works, and illustrations of events such as book burnings.

The Frontier in American Culture

The American Library Association, in cooperation with the Newberry Library in Chicago, has planned a panel exhibition, on tour from September 1996 to August 1998, on the "The Frontier in American Culture." A modular, free-standing exhibit, it will tour approximately 45 libraries.

A selection process for choosing the sites from a list of applicants for this exhibition contains the following criteria: the host library must make a commitment to delegate a staff member as coordinator who will attend an all-expenses-paid planning seminar in Chicago, and the library must plan an opening reception and other public programs in their communities. Host libraries may not charge any fees to the public to view the exhibition.

The loan period is for six weeks and the exhibition is made up of 30 panels that require 1,000–2,000 square feet of space. Host libraries receive a large banner, brochures, one copy of the catalog and a curriculum guide for secondary school teachers, 25 posters for promotion, and complete materials necessary for an ALA "Let's Talk About It" discussion group based on the theme of the exhibition.

A National Endowment for the Humanities grant covered virtually all expenses for this exhibition, including shipping and insurance. The exhibition coordinators receive a site support notebook that guides them through planning and presenting the exhibit, including a press kit and camera-ready copy for local publicity.

Exhibits from other libraries

We are all familiar with the museum exhibitions that travel from one part of the world to another. In libraries, this happens more rarely: except for those planned as traveling exhibitions, whole book exhibitions are not often borrowed. But there does not seem to be any intrinsic reason why they shouldn't be, either from another library or commercial establishment willing to lend them. And, unless an exhibition has been planned to travel, there are often no up-front fees attached.

If the borrowed exhibit is not one that was intended to travel, packing, shipping and liability matters may seem to present too many problems. But already it is common practice for libraries to borrow a few pieces or single items from either private persons or another institution for exhibit purposes. Valuable items are sometimes couriered from the lender to the borrowing library.

This could become part of exhibit planning. When your library becomes aware of a good exhibit elsewhere, especially in libraries within driving distance, a standard request form to borrow all or part could be created. It goes without saying that no library is going to be willing to lend materials unless your library is well organized and can offer guarantees of good security, handling, documentation and insurance backup. These things should be in place and a general statement regarding them on paper to send with an agreement request before you go looking for an exhibition to borrow. The following list is an approximation of the documents that you will need for this purpose. The first two categories can be taken care of by a covering letter to the incoming loan agreement.

Library information: This should include address, telephone and fax numbers, the exhibit coordinators name and e-mail address, if any. Include also a short statement about your library—how many volumes, type of library (public, special, academic, etc.), hours open, and any information about receiving materials. If the loaning institution has not already sent a form that covers exhibition space, environmental concerns such as lighting and air-conditioning, it might be well to describe these conditions.

Exhibit coordination: This should include your projected exhibit calendar for the one you propose to borrow, dates and other related events, the name and experience of your representative who has primary responsibility for exhibitions as well as anyone who will install, pack or handle the exhibit pieces.

Security statement and Loan Agreement: Supervision, facility security and alarm systems, if any, inspection routines before and after the exhibit (damage and liability control) need to be covered here. The primary emphasis, however, is on insurance. It must be clear who exactly will insure the exhibit pieces and when: in transit, during installation and demounting, and for the duration of the exhibition. If the lending institution is to insure, your library must have a copy of the insurance certificate in hand before receiving materials. On page 60 is an approximation of a Loan Agreement.

Materials checklist: Send an empty form for the lending institution to fill out regarding the actual items in the exhibit. This should include any stands, panels, tables or other supports and, most importantly, a request for the list (and the whole agreement) to be signed by the responsible person at the lending institution when agreement is reached.

WHEN IT IS BORROWING, YOUR LIBRARY MUST OFFER GUARANTEES OF GOOD SECURITY, HANDLING, DOCUMENTATION & INSURANCE BACKUP

It may be that a library that is used to lending materials will have their own set of forms that your library will have to fill out. So much the better, but it is still a good idea to have your own in case of need, to protect the library's assets if lending, and to avoid liability when borrowing. Either way, it is important to have a signed agreement in the hands of both institutions before accepting shipment of an exhibition, and to have a copy accompanying the materials. In putting together forms for borrowing and lending, to make sure that they exactly suit your library's exhibition requirements and materials, create your own.

The document on the following page is a basic form that might be used for creating both borrowing and loaning agreements. It presupposes that a complete list of the items to go on exhibit, with short annotations as to condition of the pieces, will be attached. In the case of any damage when receiving materials, a damage report should be noted on the form and attached. This form is not stated in exact legal language. When creating a permanent form, you may prefer to consult your institution's insurance carriers or risk management office.

Loaning an exhibit

Your library might usefully decide to have an exhibition program that included some exhibits that could travel. This might be in conjunction with a city-wide or state-wide program through the public library system, or it might only be loaning an exhibit to a school or local historical society. An exhibit might go to only one site or to several. Your library will have to decide if there will be a charge for the exhibit over and above shipping and handling costs or not. If the exhibition is at least partially underwritten by a patron or corporate donor, this will make it much more attractive to other libraries.

Planning an exhibit that is meant to travel: While many exhibits can be packed to travel, planning an exhibit that is meant to travel brings with it some special considerations. First and foremost is the consideration of size. For medium-sized and smaller libraries, we may assume that space and security requirements should be relatively minimal. If there are artifacts and books included, these need to be fairly sturdy, with not too many small pieces that could get lost, especially if they are to be shipped rather than couriered. Vulnerable items such as watercolors, fragile pieces, books of unusual or unique qualities should probably not be used in a traveling exhibit at all.

Photocopying has reached a sophisticated level and original pieces that should not travel such as documents, old maps, letters can be copied and even enlarged for visually powerful panels or framed mounts which travel well as in the exhibits from ALA and the Library of Congress.

Captions should be done by the lending institution and a clear set of instructions should indicate exactly which pieces go with which captions as this is not always self-evident.

Developing a Traveling Exhibit Program: If your library is interested in developing a traveling exhibit program on an ongoing basis, the same forms that are used for borrowing (incoming loans) exhibits may be revised to become the document for the institutions that will house your traveling

TEST THE SUCCESS OF AN EXHIBITION IN YOUR LIBRARY BEFORE DECIDING IT IS READY TO TRAVEL, SINCE IT WILL REQUIRE SIGNIFICANT TIME AND EFFORT TO COORDINATE exhibit. In addition, you will need a questionnaire along the lines of the one on page 61. This is not an agreement and need not be signed: it is merely an information sheet to help your library decide if the borrower can handle your exhibit appropriately. Be sure you are clear about the level of security you require for your exhibition.

Testing the success of an exhibition in your own library first is a good idea before deciding if it is ready to travel, since the coordination of such a program will require significant time on the part of the responsible person in the library of origin. They will need to:

Find host sites for the entire length of the exhibit and make sure that the space and security is adequate in each of them. If the exhibit does not have any irreplaceable materials, security may be minimal, but if a library goes to the expense of creating an exhibit, it could be a significant loss if it were vandalized or burned up in a fire.

Send the above-mentioned preliminary questionnaires and forms on security, insurance and facilities requirements, as well as a complete description of the exhibit materials so that the host institution knows exactly what to expect. A coordinator in the host institution is a must, as well. Don't forget to have a damage control form for routine inspection for condition before and after exhibit. Most lending institutions also add a request that, in the event of damage, they be contacted, and that the borrower not try to make any repairs or "fix" problems.

Include a time frame if it is important that the exhibit is there for a specific period or must be packed and mailed to another site at a certain date. Be sure to build in enough time for moving an exhibit from one site to another.

If there are valuable pieces included, send information as to how these will be shipped or if a courier will be sent with them. Even if the host institution has sufficient insurance for the exhibition while it is there, your library must nevertheless insure for travel damage if the carrier's insurance does not cover everything. It is a good idea to have insurance set up so that in the event that a host site does not have sufficient insurance, a rider can be added by a simple phone call to your usual insurance agent, followed by a letter outlining the travel dates, time frame and materials.

Packing and shipping

These are an important aspect of loaning or borrowing library materials that will be exhibited. Here again, your library's standards and regulations should be on paper, as part of the traveling exhibit program. Packing materials should be of high quality and sturdy enough to be packed and unpacked several times without undue damage. It is absolutely essential that a of list of each item sent be included in the actual box, crate or package so that it may be matched to the checklist on the receiving end.

Avoid embarrassment: Poor packing can account for major damage, especially in the case of awkward artifacts, and the library, even if insured, could be embarrassed if parts of a promised exhibit arrive broken and damaged.

Buy good quality supplies: Do not let anyone tell you that you can use popcorn to pack your library materials! Today, packing and shipping supplies may be found in every town of any size in the "pack and mail" stores. Since vibration is a travel hazard, sound packing techniques are a must. If your library is embarking on a program of traveling exhibits, such supplies can be purchased more cheaply in quantity through wholesalers. Of course, storing such materials sometimes creates space problems. Here again, perhaps the library can share expenses with another institution and not need to store large quantities at a time.

Learn packing techniques: If you do your own packing, use small containers (books are heavy!) with tops that close. Wrap each item separately, not in newspaper, but in clean paper. If the exhibition materials will not spend much time in the wrappings, clean newssheet can be used such as is found at truck rental businesses that carry moving supplies. While this paper is acidic, you may wrap one sheet of non-acid paper on the inside when an item is especially vulnerable. Books should always, without exception, be packed flat or **spine down**. If a book is set on its fore edges, the text block can simply fall out, so packing it on its spine assures that it will rest down into its case. Do not jam boxes full, but stuff spaces with extra newssheet or bubble wrap. Styrofoam peanuts can be used but they stick to everything. Whatever you use, be sure there is a thick layer on the top and the bottom of the crate too and if the boxes will be mailed, pay particular attention to the corners of the boxes. When using crates that are not solid or cardboard boxes, plastic sheets should be used as a lining.

Remember heat and humidity problems: While traveling, library materials will be under even more stress than on exhibit in your own library. Trucks can be either very hot or very cold, and humid as well. Documents may be packed in acid-free mat board or Plexiglas "sandwiches" and taped shut. They should be buffered by acid-free sheets of paper inside, or matted, in the case of anything such as maps or illustrations. Good packaging alone will help keep humidity at bay.

Security in shipping: Look into the regulations of the shipping company you plan to use. Can a shipment be traced easily? What kind of insurance is available from your carrier and how are claims made in event of damage? Are drivers responsible for the shipments, and can the trucks be locked up well in case they must leave them temporarily?

Embarking on a program of creating traveling exhibits that are permanent and can travel throughout the country is a large undertaking, and quite expensive. Nevertheless, while requiring a major commitment in staff time, such programs, especially combined with reading programs, have been well supported by the National Endowment for the Humanities and other foundations.

LOAN AGREEMENT

Exhibition Title_____

Arrival date_____ Date of Return_____

Lending Institution_____

Address_____

Insurance: Lender agrees that in the event of damage or loss, recompense will be limited to the insured amount and no further claims will be made on the borrowing institution.

Insurance by Lender_____

Insurance by Borrower_____

Date of Receipt of Certificate of Insurance_____

Special Shipping Instructions_____

_____

_____

Special Handling Instructions_____

_____

Packing & Transportation costs paid by_____

Condition as described on attached checklist of exhibition objects:

When Received_____   When Received_____

The undersigned agree that all statements in this document have been read and accepted.

Borrower_____   Lender_____
       (signature of representative)   (signature of representative)

EXHIBITION LOAN QUESTIONNAIRE

Exhibition Title_____

Loan Period_____

Lending Institution_____

Address_____

Coordinator_____   Tel. _____

Borrowing Institution_____

Address_____

Coordinator_____   Tel._____

Type of Exhibition Space_____

Environment:

    Lighting_____   UV Protection_____

    Security_____

    Maximum_____ Medium_____   Minimum_____

    Supervision_____   Fire control_____

    Air-conditioning_____   Humidity Control_____

Installation Requirements_____

_____

_____

Items Needing Special Care_____

_____

Copyright Restrictions (for items later than 1978)_____

_____

Model of a Small Exhibit of 40–50 Books

Chapter Six

In this chapter, the planning and execution of a small exhibit held in a medium-sized library is followed from beginning to end.

In 1983, for the 500th anniversary of the birth of Martin Luther, the Jesuit-Kraus-McCormick Library (JKM) in Chicago hosted a reception at the opening of an exhibit of over 40 original editions and documents from the L. Franklin Gruber Collection at the Lutheran School of Theology in Chicago. A small but very unusual collection left to the Lutheran School by a former director earlier in this century, the Gruber collection consists of several hundred items of unsurpassed rarity, primarily first editions of Luther's works, original letters, and other theological materials pertaining to the importance of Martin Luther and his writings. The exhibit was to be held in the even more unusual ecumenical setting of the three seminaries that made up the JKM Library, The Chicago Province of the Society of Jesus, The Lutheran School of Theology at Chicago, and McCormick Theological Seminary (Presbyterian).

The JKM library did not have extensive exhibit space or equipment, but did have a modest exhibit program under the direction of the Processing and Preservation Department. Mini-exhibits of ten to twenty books were continuous throughout the academic year. The library owned about four cases; others were borrowed for this special exhibit.

The exhibit planned was titled, *Luther at His Desk: Printed Works and Manuscripts from the L. Franklin Gruber Collection.* A professor from the Lutheran School of Theology acted as curator, chose the illustrations and wrote the entire text for both exhibit captions and a desk-top produced catalog and brochure. The supervisor of the library preservation and repair section coordinated the mounting and technical matters for the exhibit. Support staff from the technical services department in the library produced the computerized text for the catalog and brochure, the development office at the Lutheran School produced the catalog cover, brochures and posters for publicity purposes.

The exhibit was set in seven small flat, oblong cases on the ground floor in an air-conditioned lobby area of the library where the only public entrance is on an upper floor. The cases were locked at all times and supervision was nearly always present during library hours. The library was locked when closed and was housed in a separate wing of the seminary building where continuous reception security was maintained when open. Lighting was by sleeved fluorescent lights in a high ceiling and by daylight from large windows behind the stairwell that did not reach the exhibition cases directly. Air circulation was excellent as a curved stairwell ascended to the exhibit area from above.

Planning begins

Planning began about six months in advance. The exhibit team consisted of the faculty member curator, the preparator/coordinator and a technical services staff person from the library, and a representative of the Lutheran School development office. The curator agreed to produce a list of the pieces to be displayed and the caption materials and text in two months time and deliver immediately to the development representative the images that would be used on the cover of the exhibit catalog and posters and on a folded brochure that would include a hand-drawn map, "Luther's Europe," as well as some illustrations from some of the most famous items in the exhibit. These included the title page of the first edition of the Luther Bible, and the Papal Bull excommunicating Luther. It was decided that the brochure would be distributed free, but that there would be a small fee for the catalog except to persons invited to the opening reception and to a number of Chicago libraries to which it would be mailed.

The preparator agreed to be ready to pull the materials as soon as she received the list of items in the exhibit, to begin measuring for book supports and creating case designs.

It was decided that a banner should be hung down the staircase well to visually guide viewers to the lobby area. The large banner for the stairwell would coordinate with a textile background in the cases. The preparator would measure and purchase these. The technical services person took on the task of producing invitations to the opening reception as well as preparing the computer texts.

The two month meeting:

The reception was now planned (food was to be supplied and catered by the Lutheran School dining room), and invitations sent to representatives and faculty of two consortia of theological schools and several local libraries. The projected banners and materials were examined, and the preparator reported that all the books and manuscripts on the exhibit list were in good condition and could be exhibited safely. In a few cases of extreme rarity among individual documents, it was decided that photocopies would be used. The text of the finished captions were given to technical services where they were put on computer for the catalog and case captions. The

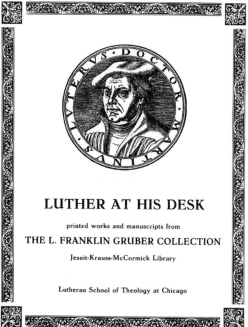

Fig. 6.1. Courtesy of the Jesuit-Krauss-McCormick Library, Chicago, Illinois.

development office representative reported that the insurance that normally covered the exhibit materials would be sufficient and that there were no new restrictions for the exhibition period provided they remained in the same part of the building (the library) where they were usually housed and kept in the locked cases.

The two week advance mark:

The brochure had been completed, the final draft of the catalog and captions were examined and approved and reception details finalized. The preparator reported that the stands and book mounts were nearly finished, and that she could now begin to mount the captions. Installation would start one day in advance of the opening reception. The building manager was invited to sit in on this meeting and security arrangements were made for the period of the reception and for occasional surveillance during regular library hours for the duration of the exhibit.

The opening:

The day before the opening, the room was cleaned, the cases moved into place and cleaned on the inside by the preparator. The textile (maroon velveteen) was laid in the cases, books were mounted on their supports and documents were placed on acid-free mat board and arranged in a sequence:

>Case I: "Early Luther, to 1519"
>Case II: "The Luther Affair: Showdown with the Papal Church"
>Cases III & IV: "Doctor of Scripture: Translator and Commentator"
>Case V & VI: "Churchman: Building up the Evangelical Church"
>Case VII: "Controversialist: the Fight for the Faith."

The cases were numbered for the convenience of viewers, and brochures and catalogs were placed in evidence.

The opening reception was held the following afternoon, with a brief greeting from the Library's director and a few words on the significance of the Luther anniversary.

Closing the exhibit:

At the conclusion of the exhibit, three months later, the preparator removed all the items from the cases, cleaned them where necessary and returned them to their special collection air-controlled vault, checking them against the original list (which included enclosures such as boxes or covers). Brochures were retained to use in the on-going church school programs that sent children to JKM Library to see a slide show and some of the Luther materials. Catalogs had sold well during the period of the exhibit and could continue to be printed up as needed from the computerized text and simply stapled into the printed cover.

The final costs of the exhibition consisted of the exhibit team staff time, the printing of the catalog cover, poster and brochure, the fabric for the banner and background, the reception invitations, food and kitchen staff, and a few hours a day of extra security.

Supplies and Services

Appendix A

Benchmark
P.O. Box 214
Rosemont, N.J. 08556
(609) 397-1159

Exhibition equipment: Butterfly Bookmounts; monitoring devices; gel tiles; fabrics; silica.

Bookbinder's Warehouse
31 Division St
Keyport, NJ 07735
(908) 264-0306

Binder's board, papers, cloth and tools.

Charles A. Dickgiesser & Co.
257 Roosevelt Drive,
Derby, CT 06418
(203) 734-2553

Manufactures and distributes the Polycase, a demountable exhibit case of clear acrylic panels.

Charrette Corporation
31 Olympic Ave
P.O.Box 4010
Woburn, MA 01888
(617) 935-6000/6010

Surface cleaning supplies, small tools, Fome-cor.

Conservation Center for Art and Historic Artifacts
264 South 23rd St
Philadelphia,Pa. 19103
(215) 545-0613

Conservation of paper, books and artifacts.

Dickson Instruments Co.
930 S. Westwood Dr.
Addison, Ill 60101
(312) 543-3747

Hygrothermographs for measuring humidity and temperature; light meters.

Highsmith Inc.
W5527 Hwy. 106
Fort Atkinson, WI 53538-0800
1-800-558-2110

General library supplies and book repair materials; display cases.

Hollinger Corporation
P.O.Box 8360
Frederickburg, VA 22404-8360
1-800-634-0491

Polyester film encapsulation supplies; map folders; photographic sleeves; archival storage boxes.

Kool View Co., Inc,
2503A West Beltline Highway,
Madison, WI. 53713
(608) 273-4224.

Ultraviolet protective window treatments: film & glazes for exhibit cases.

LBS\Archival Products
2134 East Grand Ave
P.O.Box 1413
Des Moines, IA 50305
(515) 262-3191

Archival quality book board, folders, binders and enclosures.

Light Impressions
439 Monroe Ave.
P.O. Box 940
Rochester, NY 14603-0904
1-800-828-6216

Photographic supplies; albums, display mats and mounts; UV light filters; air purifiers and humidity monitors; polyester film envelopes for encapsulation.

New England Document Conservation Center
100 Brickstone Square
Andover, MA 01810-1494
(508) 470-1010

National library/archive conservation services and consultation; technical conservation leaflets, including suppliers list.

Solar Screen Co
53-11 105th St
Corona, NY 11368
(212) 592-8222

EZ-Bond UV protective clear sheets; fluorescent bulb UV protection jackets.

TALAS
213 West 35th St
New York, NY 10001-1996
(212) 736-7744

Acid-free papers, bookbinding supplies; tools and humidity indicators; exhibit and display cases.

United Foam Plastics Corporation
172 East Main St
Georgetown, MA 01833-2107

Foam wedges for book supports (Wilford Polyforms).

University Products, Inc
517 Main St.
P.O.Box 101
Holyoke, MA 01041-0101
1-800-762-1165

Every type of archival quality storage container; acrylic book cradles and supports; standing display panels; papers, mat board, some tools and environmental monitors.

Wisconsin Preservation Program
Kathy Schneider, Director
728 State St
Madison, WI 53706
(608) 273-2773

Free preservation advice; limited books, pamphlets, and environmental monitors for regional loan.

Encapsulation of Single-Sheet Documents

Appendix B

Materials needed:

> polyester film (Mylar-type D)
> double-faced tape (3-M brand #415,
> $1/4"$–$1/2"$ depending on size of document)
> weights (one or more, depending on the size of document)
> utility knife
> scissors
> Squeegee (optional)

Instructions:

1. Cut two pieces of polyester film at least 1" larger than the document on all sides.

2. Place the paper document **between** the two sheets of polyester and center it.

3. Put one or more weights on the "sandwich" to hold layers in place.

4. On the upper surface of the top polyester sheet, apply tape to the film, "framing" the document below and making sure to leave a $1/8"$ space

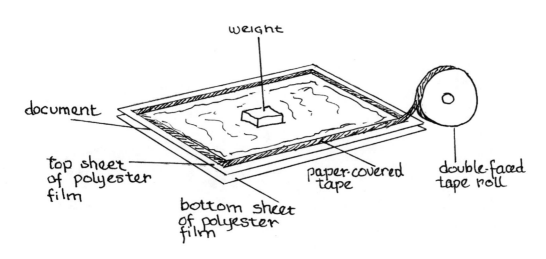

between the edge of the document and the edge of the tape.

At three of the corners, the ends of the tape may be butted against each other at right angles; at the fourth corner a small gap may be left between the edges to allow for release of air.

Leave the brown protective paper on the tape.

Note: For documents that have not been deacidified, the tape may be left off of one entire side of the frame.

5. Place the taped polyester sheet on a flat surface and check carefully for any stray pieces of lint, dust, etc. Clean thoroughly with a lint-free cloth.
6. Center the document inside the tape frame.
7. Thoroughly clean the second sheet of polyester and place it on top of the first sheet, sandwiching the document.
8. Apply weight(s).
9. Carefully lift one corner of the top sheet of film to expose two strips of tape.

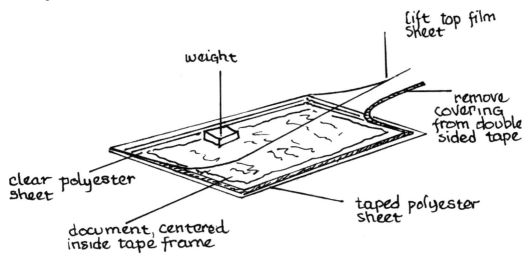

10. Pull paper backing from the exposed strips of tape.
11. Allow polyester to fall back into place. Smooth carefully from center outward with a Squeegee or with your hand to remove excess air.
12. Repeat steps 9–11 for remaining sides of document.
13. With scissors or utility knife, trim off excess polyester film, making sure to leave approximately $1/8$" of film beyond the outer edge of the tape.
14. Corners may be mitred with scissors or rounded with a mechanical device.

Small Workstation for Exhibit Preparation

Appendix C

The construction of a small workstation where books may be measured, boxes made, repairs completed and supplies stored for all of these activities need not be very large. The drawing below suggests a long workbench at which work is done standing up rather than sitting, but this is optional. A lower bench may be adapted as well. Flat storage for large paper and binder's board and card stock, textiles and other materials used in exhibit work may be kept below the high counter, and at one end. A small amount of cupboard space is sufficient for glues, pastes, and other small items. Some basic tools and supplies usually needed for minor book repair and handwork are listed.

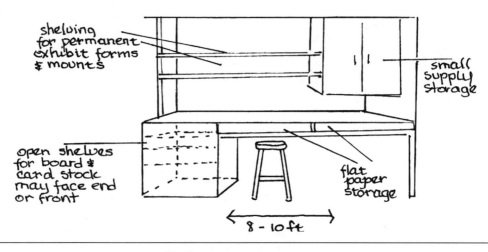

Supplies:

polyvinyl acetate adhesive (PVA glue)

archival document repair paper tape

binder's book cloth

polyester film sheets or roll for encapsulation

clean waste paper (newssheet) for gluing up

binder's board or card stock

acid-neutral papers

Tools:

mat knife	tweezers
cork-backed rulers, 12" to 24"	bone folders
	cleaning cloths
round glue bristle brushes, several sizes	heavy weights
fine lead pencil	small embroidery scissors
large shears	

Glossary

acknowledgment credit or thanks to be included in captions or written recognition of assistance

acid-free pH neutral (pH 7) or greater

acidic below pH neutral

alkaline greater than pH neutral

annotation additional written information, comment or explanation of a specific written item

artifact the physical item; the structure of an object

binder's board a dense cardboard used for bookbinding

book structure the physical arrangement of the parts of a book

book support a construction to hold a book in a specific position

caption the label accompanying and explaining the importance of a specific item on exhibit or used in an exhibition catalog for the same purpose

conservation the treatment given to library materials to repair, preserve or restore them

conservation facility a laboratory or workshop for library materials conservation

conservator a person trained in the treatment and repair of specific materials and artifacts

courier a person designated to accompany exhibition materials from one place to another destination

disaster plan a plan to cover prevention, preparedness, action and recovery in the event of a disaster

dpt program computer program for desk top publishing

encapsulation an enclosure or envelope made of polyester film

endorsement *see rider*

exhibit an integral display or presentation

exhibition a group of related exhibits or an organized presentation of multiple items

grid an arbitrary division of a page into rectangles

hygrothermograph an instrument that measures both temperature and humidity

installation the preparing and placing of exhibition materials in exhibit cases

lux international light measure (one lumen per square meter, or .0929 footcandles)

micro-climate an enclosed atmosphere or environment

mini-exhibit an exhibit of fewer than 20 books or documents

off-gas releasing of gasses into the atmosphere

particulate matter infinitesimal dust-like particles

pasteup the final layout of materials that are given to the printer for printing

preparator the person who prepares the exhibition space, background materials and cases, as well as the physical arranging of the books and documents for exhibition

preservation the actions or decisions made to extend the life of library materials

Rh relative humidity

rider a legal, binding addition to a current insurance policy

security the assurance of physical and environmental safety for library materials

UV ultraviolet light

vitrines small, free standing glass cases

Selected Bibliography

Adler, Elizabeth W. *Everyone's Guide to Successful Publications*, Berkeley, CA: Peach-pit Press, 1993.

Baker, Mary. "Safe Plastics for Storage and Display," *Washington Conservation Guild Newsletter*, November, 1990, 4-5.

Barford, Michael. "Environmental Monitoring Just Got Easier," *Abbey Newsletter*, 15:6 (1991), 92.

Block, Huntington T. "Insurance: An Integral Part of Your Security Dollar." *Museum News*, 50:5 (1972), 26-29.

Bowen, Laura G. and Roberts, Peter J. "Exhibits: Illegitimate Children of Academic Libraries?" *College and Research Libraries News*, 54(1993), 407-415.

Casterline, Gail F. *Archives & Manuscripts: Exhibits.* Chicago: Society of American Archivists, 1980, 8.

Caswell, Lucy S. "Building a Strategy for Academic Library Exhibits." *C&RL News*, 46 (1985), 165-68.

Chapman, Joseph. "Fire." *Museum News*, January, 1972, 32-35.

Culp, R.W. "Thefts...." *Special Libraries* 67:11 (1976) 582-84.

Dolloff, Francis, and Perkinson, Roy L. *How to Care For Works of Art on Paper*, 3rd ed. Boston: Museum of Fine Arts, 1979.

Erickson, Erika. "Book and Manuscript Support Systems," presentation at the symposium, "The Making of the Lincoln Exhibition" at the Huntington Library, San Marino, CA April, 1994.

Jones, Dorothy E. and Grosch, Mary. "Exhibits Speak Louder Than Words." *Technicalities*, 7:9, (1986), 6

Kemp, Jane. "Creating Exhibits in Smaller Academic Libraries," *C&RL News*, 46, (1985), 344-346.

Korley, Marie, "Exhibition Catalogues," *The Papers of the Bibliographical Society of America*, 79:4 (1985) 543-566

Markoff, Marjorie, "More than Innovation: A Popular Exhibit Shows the Personal Side of Books and Information," in "Innovations," *C&RL News*, 49, (1988), 367-68.

Nicholson, Catherine "What Exhibits Can Do to Your Collection." *Restaurator*, 13:(1992), 95-113.

Protection of Libraries and Library Collections, #910, Quincy, MA, National Fire Protection Agency, 1991

Research Libraries Group, Inc. *RLG Preservation Manual,* "Exhibits," 2nd ed., 1986, 140-42.

Schaeffer, Mark. *Library Displays Handbook.* New York: H.W. Wilson Co., 1991

Schull, Dorothy Dow. "Shhh...owtime at the Library: Exhibits Lend New Life to Old Institutions." *Museum News,* 63:4 (1985) 36-41.

Stolow, Nathan. *Conservation and Exhibitions: Packing, Transport, Storage and Environmental Considerations.* Boston, Butterworths, 1987

Thompson, Garry. *The Museum Environment.* Boston: Butterworths, 1978

Williams, Robin, *The Non-Designer's Design Book.* Berkeley, CA: Peachpit Press, 1994.

Wyly, Mary, ed. "Exhibits in ARL Libraries," SPEC Kit #120, Washington, D.C: Association of Research Libraries Office of Management Studies, 1981.

To subscribe to an electronic list on library exhibits:

Exhibits and Displays in Libraries
list name: LIBEX-L
send message to subscribe:
"Subscribe LIBEX-L your name" to
LIBEX-L@MAINE@NU021140@NDSUVM1
address: NU021140@NDSUVM1

Index